American Pickup Trucks
of the 1950s

Also from Veloce:

Veloce Publishing's other imprints:

 A range of quality books about military history

 www.hubbleandhattie.com
A range of quality books dedicated to animal welfare

eBooks and Apps available from www.digital.veloce.co.uk

For post publication news, updates and amendments relating to this book please visit www.veloce.co.uk/books/V4802

www.veloce.co.uk

First published in March 2016 by Veloce Publishing Limited, Veloce House, Parkway Farm Business Park, Middle Farm Way, Poundbury, Dorchester DT1 3AR, England. Fax 01305 268864 / e-mail info@veloce.co.uk / web www.veloce.co.uk or www.velocebooks.com. ISBN 978-1-845848-02-6; UPC 6-36847-04802-0.

Contents

Preface

In this 12th motoring book published along with my son, Andrew Mort, we have once again combined his many photographic skills and my knowledge, research and writing to tell the fascinating story of the evolution of the American ½-ton pickup truck in the 1950s.

Andrew personally handled all the images – scanning, enhancing, cropping, recording, filing and packaging, as well as accompanying me on trips shooting and collecting information. He was also responsible for most of the color shots of the restored trucks.

In addition to our images there are many pickup truck enthusiasts and collectors such as longtime International dealer, George Kirkham (Southland International Trucks Ltd), who provided full access to his private collection of International pickups, including a rare 1957 Golden Jubilee A-100.

From the Studebaker Driver's Club, members Mark Hayden (1957 Transtar) ½-ton pickup, and Joseph and Hilda Benincasso (1954 3R5), who kindly contributed photographs.

Also, numerous collector car and truck dealers in the United States were very supportive of our project. This included Country Classic Cars (1957 Ford Ranchero), and Mark Hyman and Shawn Dougan of Hyman Motors Ltd Classic Cars (1950 Studebaker).

Bill Peeters of Bill's Truck Stop in Ontario also provided numerous shots and assistance with rare optional 1950s pickup truck equipment.

Andrew and I would also like to thank Rod Grainger, and his knowledgeable team at Veloce Publishing, for their continuing encouragement and faith in our endeavors.

American ½-ton pickup trucks were built for a rugged life. Despite the daily toil until something finally broke, many were saved for future repair. For some this still has not come – such is the case with this mid-fifties GMC. (N Mort Collection)

Introduction

In the 1950s the term ½-ton was applied to the range of light, practical trucks based on the maximum load carrying capacity of 1000lb (453.5kg). The load capacity referred to the maximum amount of weight these light trucks' springs, chassis, and bed were designed to carry. By the end of the decade most ½-ton pickup trucks had been developed to the point where it was safe to carry about 500lb (227kg) more. This was also based on the Gross Vehicle Weight Rating (GVWR) noted by the manufacturer. The GVWR included the curb weight, additional equipment that had been added, the weight of cargo and the weight of passengers.

Whereas most of the pickup trucks built prior to 1950 were strictly utilitarian vehicles, designed for city business hauling or the daily chores of farm living, the postwar era ½-ton pickup trucks quickly improved in sophistication, comfort, and performance. Later in the decade, the ½-ton pickup trucks would be treated to a high-style look with the addition of lots of chrome, trim, many comfort and convenience options, and painted in two and three-tone pastel colors. The American manufacturers correctly read the evolving changes in the postwar marketplace, which paid immediate dividends, and the ½-ton pickup trucks would go on to become the best-selling vehicles in North America.

As the decade progressed, the ½-ton pickup truck played a major role in the increasing entrepreneurship of the burgeoning American middle class. With the continued boom in such areas as construction – from plazas and office towers to industrial buildings and suburban homes – trucks of all sizes were required. Small businesses also need trucks – and here is where the ½-ton pickup truck, in particular, came into its element, whether to help install swimming pools, construct patios or family recreation rooms, or for gardening projects, etc. The ½-ton pickup truck was seen as being ideally suited to the needs of this steadily increasing number of independent local businesses.

At the same time, these tough and reliable pickup trucks were about to play an important role in America's newly discovered interest in travel, cottages and camping, thanks to the opening of new interstate highways. While the next generation of station wagons met the needs of many American families, it was the ½-ton pickup truck that was perfect for heavier loads and the towing of boats and travel trailers to enjoy recreational living to its fullest.

In this more affluent decade, eventually a pickup truck would become a familiar sight, parked in the ever-increasing new suburban household driveways. By the end of the decade the pickup truck would quickly evolve into an acceptable second – or even first – family transport vehicle in North American neighborhoods.

Demand for these handy pickup trucks was strong throughout the fifties, and to meet that challenge the American-designed, dual-purpose work and family ½-ton pickup trucks were built in a wide range of models, providing a variety of sizes, drivetrains, styles and comfort levels.

Today, these 1950s dual-purpose work and family pickup truck designs, developed for the new era buyers throughout the decade, have become iconic symbols to American vintage truck collectors.

Not included in this volume are the 4x4 versions

The 1950s in North America was famous for colorful, chrome-adorned and flamboyantly-styled automobiles, and this was often carried over into truck designs, as is evident in this well-optioned, two-tone, 1955 Chevrolet 3100 Series Step-Side ½-ton. (N Mort Collection)

of the ½-ton pickup trucks offered. These began to appear in the 1950s with aftermarket, factory approved conversions from Marmon-Herrington, NAPCO, etc. As the decade ended the conversions were to become factory-installed.

Through the use of rarely seen cut-away drawings, never before published photographs of fully restored trucks, and images sourced from period advertisements and brochures, this volume covers all the major light-

duty American ½-ton pickup trucks built in the decade of the 1950s.

The non-conventional ½-ton pickup trucks such as the Chevrolet El Camino and Ford Ranchero, along with the rarer Fargo and Mercury models have also been included.

The detailed text describes the annual model changes and highlights distinctive styling cues. Also, many of the engine and chassis specifications have been inserted where relevant, along with the significant industry production facts and figures. In addition we have included a quick look at today's customizing trends for these trucks, as well as a detailed look at five of the most popular or unusual pickup truck models of the 1950s.

And finally, there is a chapter focusing on 1950s pickup truck options. While many of these added features often became standard equipment in the years that followed, some were incredibly unique and unusual at the time.

Old work trucks like this 1951 GMC ½-ton pickup have become family heirlooms to many enthusiasts. (Courtesy Bill's Truck Shop)

Into a new decade – a brave new world!

The prewar pickup truck market in America was very different from the one that was emerging in peacetime. In the immediate years following WWII some makes did not return to the market, while the major builders initially carried on with prewar designs.

As the 1930s unfolded and the Great Depression dragged along, there were many automakers and truck companies that felt by diversifying into new potential sales areas they could stave off bankruptcy.

Even though Chrysler Corporation was successfully marketing its Dodge and Fargo line-up of trucks in the thirties, including ½-ton pickups, the company decided to add a Plymouth version for sale through its Chrysler-Plymouth and DeSoto-Plymouth dealerships.

Having been newly introduced in 1928, the

Ford and its 'hungry for new' customers settled for mildly updated prewar designs, until the all-new pickup arrived in 1948. The new 1948 Ford ½-ton pickup truck is credited with saving the ailing Ford Motor Company. (Courtesy Ford Motor Company)

Plymouth car line was Chrysler's entry in the low-priced field. Such was the make's success that by 1931 the Plymouth was the third most popular automobile in the United States.

As a result, the 116in wheelbase Plymouth PT-50 pickup truck was introduced in 1937. Alas, its first year would prove to be its most popular in the long run.

The new pickup was part of a commercial line-up that also included a sedan delivery, a station wagon, and a cab and chassis combination. By 1939, the Plymouth had adapted the all-new Dodge styling and design with some of its own unique cues and trim.

With only minor trim and grille changes, Plymouth pickup trucks continued to be sold until 1941. Already building military vehicles by that time, there was no Plymouth pickup planned for 1942, and subsequently no Plymouth trucks were reintroduced following the war.

Elsewhere, major truck builder Mack had also introduced a line of pickup trucks in the thirties. In 1936 through to 1938 the long-established US automaker REO reinvented itself solely as a truck manufacturer – near the end of its car production in 1935 the company had excess production capacity, and, as a result, the first Mack pickup trucks were assembled by REO.

Mack went on to build its own line of pickup trucks in 1938, but met with little success. In fact, production of these lighter trucks peaked in 1941 at just 707 units, while most of the light truck units Mack built during the war were fire pumpers.

The light truck line was dropped by 1945, since all possible production capacity was required to meet the pent-up demand for large civilian trucks. Thus, Mack abandoned the light truck market forever.

REO had begun building a line of light trucks in 1911, and between 1915 and 1926 built its original, and ultimately famous, REO Speedwagon. The name continued to be used in its truck line into the 1930s.

REO introduced a new ½-ton pickup truck in 1935, which continued into the 1940s, yet volume sales failed to materialize. Only 1-ton trucks were offered after the war into the early 1950s, based on the REO 1½-ton models.

The American Bantam evolved from American Austin, which built cars based on the popular, diminutive British Austin Seven. Commercial vehicles were introduced in 1937 in the form of a panel delivery and a tiny ¼-ton pickup truck. These models remained basically unchanged in appearance until production was halted in 1940. Austin Bantam models never surpassed 900 units, and fell to a mere 400 in its final year.

Bantam is best remembered today as the original designer of the American Jeep. Due to its lack of production capacity throughout the war, Bantam built only trailers. Production of these trailers continued after the war until 1956. Neither car nor truck production had resumed when the company was acquired by Armco Steel.

Although not all of these makes offered pickup trucks following WWII, there were some smaller manufacturers that introduced new pickup trucks for the postwar market.

Hudson had never been a major manufacturer of pickup trucks, despite the fact that in 1929 the firm had established Dover as the company's commercial division. The line-up of four different Dover trucks failed to attract buyers. The name was dropped by the end of the 1932 model year after only 4328 examples had been sold. The commercial division was then put under the Essex Terraplane nameplate, but only 400 were built in 1933, and so the Essex name was dropped in favor of

Hudson was never a major player in the pickup truck market in North America, but the high demand for new trucks following the war was enough reason to continue with its late 1930s design. (N Mort Collection)

just Terraplane. The Terraplane was a unique truck at the time, as it was a unibody design.

Hudson offered a very car-like looking ½-ton pickup truck after WWII. Although stylish, production of the six-cylinder truck was halted in 1947 forever.

Nash had built trucks over the years, and, following WWII, continued building larger models on wheelbases of 133in and 157in, but soon dropped out of the market. A number of postwar prototype pickups were built utilizing Nash automobile front ends, engines and frames. The half dozen built in 1948 were used around the plant in Kenosha for a number of years.

Following the war, new cars were in huge demand, and Nash saw this as a far more profitable market in the long run. Today, a few Nash ½-ton pickups survive in the hands of enthusiasts. No Nash pickup trucks were built in the 1950s – the company did build semis and 2½-ton trucks (4998 units) from 1948 to 1954, but not after the Hudson (AMC) merger.

There were also manufacturers who felt there was a market for smaller pickup trucks. Crosley was actually one of the smallest automobile manufacturers in the US, and yet felt there were enough reasons for the additional design and engineering expenses to enter the ¼-ton pickup market.

In the past, Powel Crosley Jr had been immensely successful at whatever he had attempted. He was an inventor, and, by 1922, Crosley was the world's largest radio manufacturer, and had established 'The Nation's Station' in Cincinnati.

Crosley went on to manufacture kitchen appliances, and filed the patent for shelves in refrigerator doors. In 1934 he added the Cincinnati Reds to the Crosley Radio Corporation.

On April 29th, 1939, at the Indianapolis Speedway, Crosley realized his longtime automotive dream and introduced his tiny 'Car of Tomorrow.' This was a $300 Austin Seven-sized car, available as a sedan, station wagon, convertible, and ¼-ton pickup truck.

Total Crosley sales rose steadily to 2289 units in 1941, and over 1000 were sold in early 1942 before production halted when America entered WWII.

Following WWII, the Crosley reappeared with fresh postwar styling, and production in 1947 exceeded 19,000 units. It rose to 28,734 units in 1948 – which included an industry-high number of approximately 20,000 station wagons.

A major design flaw in the engine, combined with an increasingly larger number of full-size secondhand cars, resulted in a dramatic decline in sales.

For 1949 a new engine was designed, but, despite this, Crosley production sank below 8000 units, and continued to tumble. By 1951 sales averaged just 6000 units annually, so in May 1952 Crosley decided to halt production, including its ¼-ton pickup. The car company was acquired by General Tire and Rubber that year. General Tire and Rubber then merged with Aerojet, and the Crosley factory was outfitted for the production of rocket parts.

Even later into the decade, the rarely heard of Powell station wagons and ¼-ton pickups were introduced in 1955-56. Brothers Hayward and Channing Powell of California first made a name for themselves as builders of first motor scooters, and then motorhomes.

The later Powell pickups and station wagons were unusual because of their origins. The vehicles were built on old scrapped, Plymouth 117in chassis that were completely rebuilt or refurbished.

All of the Powell pickup trucks and station wagons were powered by rebuilt 1940-1950 Chrysler, Desoto, Dodge, or Plymouth six-cylinder engines, rated at around 90bhp. A three-speed synchromesh transmission was fitted, along with an independent, coil spring front suspension. The unique slab body pre-dated Chevy's much-acclaimed Cameo Carrier, but its bland fiberglass front end did nothing to generate sales. Priced at $250 less than its closest competitor, this ¼-ton pickup sold relatively well, considering its origins and lightweight capabilities.

Sold almost exclusively in the United States, over 1000 pickups and 300 station wagons were built. Some of the unsold Powell wagons and trucks were ultimately registered as 1957 models.

While other larger American truck manufacturers would offer a ¼-ton pickup over the next two decades, it wasn't until the 1970s that demand for a 'mini' truck created a hot new market.

And thus, as America entered the very competitive, fast-growing pickup truck market of the 1950s, there were only a handful of well-established contenders, which included Ford, General Motors, Chrysler, Studebaker, International Harvester, and Willys (Jeep).

Most Canadian-built Mercury pickup trucks were fancier than their Ford counterparts. This fully restored 1947 1800B model became even more stylish when sold with added optional chrome, front signal lamps, and a side-mounted spare.
(N Mort Collection)

Chevrolet quickly resumed production of its prewar pickup truck to meet the postwar demand. Pictured is a 1946 1300 Series ½-ton, powered by Chevrolet's 216.5ci OHV straight six.
(N Mort Collection)

'Ford tough' for over a century!

Ford can trace the history of its factory-built pickup trucks back to 1917, when the Model T was the basis of its line-up. (Courtesy Ford Motor Company)

On June 16, 1903 Henry Ford established the Ford Motor Company and built the Model A. Some of these early chassis were fitted with non-factory, 'aftermarket' commercial bodies, but in October, 1904 Ford decided to build the Model E Delivery Car. Focusing on car production, only ten of these trucks were built in 1905, and it wasn't until 1917 that Ford built another 'factory' truck.

At that point, Ford introduced the Model TT, designed specifically as a truck. It marked the beginning of a tradition and standard that has continued to this day. The Model TT featured a heavy-duty frame and longer wheelbase for greater strength and flexibility, a stiffer rear suspension with reinforced wheels, special tires and wheels to handle heavy payloads, a sturdier rear axle for tough hauling, and front end styling to complement Ford's passenger car design.

By 1923 over 225,000 Ford trucks were built in North America and by 1924 Ford was delivering factory fitted, all-steel truck bodywork with an open pickup-type box on the Model TT chassis in three styles.

On April 15th, 1925 came the introduction of Ford's first lightweight American pickup, and in 1928, in celebration of Ford Motor Company's 25th Anniversary, came the introduction of the Model AA truck line.

The new 1932 Model BB Ford trucks helped highlight the introduction of V8 power, parallel semi-elliptic rear springs, and an enlarged fuel tank repositioned below the seat for greater safety.

Ford's 1948 'Bonus Built' trucks helped set the struggling Ford Motor Company back on its feet, as much as the highly heralded, and most often credited, all-new 1949 Ford car line. (Courtesy Ford Motor Company)

Following WWII, Ford's first all-new postwar vehicle was a truck. The 1948 'Bonus Built' pickup trucks were offered in 139 variations and would be known as the F-Series. Ford's F-Series ½-ton pickup trucks set new standards for the industry. This latest pickup truck also helped Ford regain its market share and put the company back on the road to prosperity.

In fact, the Ford F-Series truck lineup, now in its 66th year, has been the best-selling truck in America for 37 consecutive years, and the best-selling vehicle in America for 32 consecutive years. In Canada, the F-series has been the best-selling truck for 48 consecutive years, and the best-selling vehicle for four consecutive years.

Ford – from 'Bonus Built' to 'Driverized' to ...

The Bonus Built pickup truck introduced in 1948 was revolutionary in design compared to its carried-over, prewar predecessor. In styling alone, it was a dramatic change. The windscreen was one piece of glass, the

The new 1948 'Million Dollar' cab featured many firsts that were utilized on the entire Ford truck line-up by 1950, and even 50 years later can be seen in this 1998 F150. By 1950 only a few visual changes had been made in trim, colors and badging. The runningboards were also altered slightly, yet production in 1950 reached a total of 148,956 ½-ton pickup trucks alone, exceeding the entire Ford truck production total of 1948 by 10,000 units. (Courtesy Ford Motor Company)

headlamps were recessed into the front grille, the spare tire removed from the side and hidden under the box, and the hood and front fenders flattened on top. With its 3in wider stance, the new F-Series provided a distinctive, cleaner and more modern look.

The all-steel cab was quieter, taller, wider and longer, as well as being mounted with rubber levers and bushings for less vibration.

Known as the F-1, all the pickups were shod in painted black steel wheels, and, across both the car and truck line-up, wore a standard chrome Ford hubcap.

Comfort and convenience features included an ashtray, vent window and cowl ventilation, a glovebox, a 3-speed synchromesh transmission and a 6½ft box.

The tried and true 95hp, 226.4 six-cylinder engine with a single-barrel carburettor was offered as standard, or buyers could opt for the equally reliable 100hp, 239.4ci Flathead V8.

By 1950 Ford had made a only a few small noticeable exterior changes on its popular F-1 pickup truck, such as attaching the runningboards directly to the frame, as well as the supports, the vent window trim changed to black paint, new F-100 badges, and the steel wheels were now a match to the body color.

Likewise, inside there were minor alterations and color changes, with the most significant being a more comfortable and adjustable seat, and the change to the 3-speed transmission becoming a column shift.

The new look in 1951 is best described as 'different,' with its toothy-looking, 'dagmar' uprights. The name is based on a military term for the shape of shells (a 40mm self-propelled anti-aircraft tank, dubbed the Dagmar Twin 40s) or by some, from the busty shape of television personality Virginia Ruth Egnor, who was also known as Dagmar. (Andrew Mort)

In 1951 Ford refreshed its F-1 with new front end styling. The toothy-looking, horizontal grille and headlamp consisted of a combination of 'dagmar' uprights. Above this unique grille treatment were three narrow horizontal slots which were repeated again, directly above, in chrome in the hood. New, bold chrome trim and badging also graced the sides of the hood. The front fender line was different and the bumper was given a trimmer look by being ribbed.

Production dropped significantly to just 117,414 pickup trucks despite the cosmetic changes and improvements made to the engines and the transmission.

For 1952 the most noticeable difference was the grille, which was now a standard white, and the hubcaps – and later in the year the rear taillight bezels – switched from chrome to Argent Silver. These were concessions because of the limited availability of materials, due to the Korean Conflict. The badges, nameplate, tiny hood grille

In 1951, the long, bright chrome, spear-shaped hood trim and Ford nameplate were hardly subtle. The rear box was redesigned and featured squared corners and a grain-tight tailgate. A wooden floor was standard on the 6½ft box. (Andrew Mort)

On earlier 1950s pickup trucks the dagmars were painted or finished in Argent Silver, but this was later changed due to the reduction in the use of chrome because of the Korean Conflict. The remaining 1951 models and all of the 1952 dagmar grilles were painted in a cream color. (Andrew Mort)

Even in 1952 a Ford Pickup could be fashionable. Two-tone red and black paintwork, nice chrome touches, and options such as step-plates, a front chrome bumper and wide whitewall tires all provided plenty of pizazz. (Andrew Mort)

and side spears were also modified slightly. The big news was under the hood, with an all-new, 215ci six cylinder engine replacing the old L-head Six.

Another new grille – with some added chrome headlamp rims – in 1953 provided a cleaner, overall more modern appearance, whilst being more in keeping with Ford's car styling.

Other changes included a wider, flatter, lower hood, new Ford badging, and more added chrome trim on the Deluxe models. New designations saw the ½-ton pickups becoming the F-100, with the ¾-ton and 1-ton now labelled the F-250 and F-500 respectively.

Inside there was improved, wider seating, as well as a slightly overall more spacious, comfortable and luxurious 'Driverized Cab.' Overall vision was improved with a larger greenhouse. All Ford trucks featured a company 50th anniversary horn button.

The pickup box was also re-engineered, and the heftier rear tailgate now spelled-out Ford in block letters, rather than the traditional script. A change in chassis thinking saw the front axle being pushed rearward by 4in (10cm) from its previous position. Customers were impressed and bought 116,437 F-100 pickup trucks.

For 1954 there were more front end and minor

SWING open the new wider doors! Door handles are the easy-operating, push-button type . . . the kind you get on quality cars. Door latches are new rotor-type.

HOIST your size 12's into the cab! There's plenty of room between the seat and door pillar. No need to do a toe dance getting into or out of a Ford "DRIVERIZED CAB"!

SLIDE into the wide, comfortable seat. Bounce on it to test the super-cushioning action of Ford's exclusive seat shock snubber and new non-sag seat springs.

GLANCE back through the 4-ft. rear window. Heads right, or heads left, (without leaning) you can see the space you're backing into. Why pay extra for rear quarter windows?

STRETCH your arms into big cab roominess. With more hip-room than any of the 5 other leading truck makes, FORD DRIVERIZED CABS banish that "squeezed-in" feeling.

SIGH a sigh of real contentment! Man! What a treat for a working guy! And it's all yours in the new Ford DRIVERIZED CAB . . . the world's most comfortable truck cab.

1953 saw some of the most significant changes made to date, with Ford's new 'Driverized Cab' the big headline. The new cab design featured wider doors, lots of footroom to ease getting in, a wide comfortable seat, more hiproom, a 4ft-wide rear window, and vastly improved overall comfort. Ford advertising challenged potential buyers to take the 'Ford 15-second Sit Down Test.' (N Mort Collection)

cosmetic trim and badging changes. The grille design saw the return of two dagmar uprights, but the overall look was supposedly to mimic a jet wing. Production slid to just 101,202 ½-ton pickups.

1955 saw yet another new winged grille dominated by a large Vee-shape, painted this year in an off-white rather than the previous cream. The V8s were still immediately identifiable by a chrome V, and the six-cylinder models by a 4-pointed star. Deluxe F-100 trucks continued to feature added chrome trim and more

Ford had introduced its overhead valve, light-duty truck engine in 1952. The 101hp, 215ci 'Cost Clipper' four main bearing, six-cylinder engine had a compression ratio of 7.0:1 and produced 185lb-ft of torque, which was considered high. Special emblems noted Ford's 50th anniversary. The company also built its 40 millionth vehicle that year. (N Mort Collection)

Likewise, the 1953 Mercury was restyled, although the difference between the two brands was even less than before, apart from badging. The Canadian Mercury pickups were still being fitted with the old L-Head six-cylinder engine, rather than the new OHV six. Ford reportedly invested four years of R&D, and over 30 million dollars, in the new 1953 F-100/Mercury 'Ford Economy Trucks.' (N Mort Collection)

For 1954 the Ford F-100 was powered by the first-year-offered new Y-Block, 130hp, 239ci, OHV V8 engine. Fitted with a Holley 2-bbl carburettor, this more powerful V8 was rated at 214lb-ft of torque @ 1800-2200rpm, and replaced the old, but venerable, Flathead engine that dated back to 1932. (Andrew Mort)

standard features. The V8 saw a miniscule 2hp increase to 132hp. Total production reached 124,842 pickups.

After three years of minor styling changes and engineering improvements, the F-100 was completely face-lifted in 1956, and its running gear uprated, despite the fact it would be all-new in 1957.

While the four fenders and hood remained basically unchanged, the new grille virtually filled the front end completely to become much more integrated into the overall design. Rather than being painted off-white, the 'Custom Cab' package included a chromed grille, which was the first to appear on a Ford truck since 1938.

The fully reconfigured 1956 cab was responsible for the fresher look. The wrap-around windscreen, restyled vent windows, doors and roof.

The soon popular 'Custom Cab' option included both cosmetic and practical added features, from chrome trim to upgraded, more stylish materials. A dome light, a right-hand armrest, dual horns and other features were now standard equipment on all F-100s. An unusual option – and very rarely seen today – was a larger rear window which included chrome trim, and for the front screen too.

As was the custom, the badges, trim, etc, were modified, and a special 'Fordomatic' script added when the F-100 was fitted with the optional automatic transmission.

Yet, the big news was the 167hp, 273ci 'Power King' V8 that had finally funneled down to the ½-ton pickups. The 133hp, 223ci six was still offered as the base engine.

1956 F-100 styling was more distinctive than its predecessors, despite it being the last year for this model. New safety innovations included a deep-dish steering wheel and optional panoramic rear window. (Courtesy Ford Motor Company)

Also new for '56 was a standard 12-volt system, tubeless tires and a choice of ten colors, plus two-toning combinations paired with Colonial White.

The base F-100 came with a 6ft box, or was available with an 8ft box. This model was called the F-100 Express, and utilized the frame from the heftier F-250. Pickup production continued to increase steadily in 1956, with 137,581 units delivered.

The highly angular, sculptured form of the F-100 was a dramatic change in 1957, with no longer any

The new Styleside body was offered at no extra cost in 1957, and promoted as the largest in the ½-ton field, providing 24 percent more load space. Both the Styleside and more traditional Flareside were available in 6½ft or 8ft box sizes. All the Styleside models had a steel box floor, whereas the Flaresides had wooden floors. (N Mort Collection)

separate fenders front or rear, and no runningboards. The cab was now fully integrated into the styling. Yet, the biggest news was the standard 'Styleside' model featuring smooth-sided rear fenders and box.

Although this flat-sided styling had first been seen on GM's 1955 Chevrolet and GMC trucks, it had only been offered as an option on its most expensive models.

While GM used the same narrow box on its smooth-sided models, Ford's smooth-sided box both inside and out was a huge feature. Ford's pickup trucks now had an additional 45 percent more loadspace. The traditional narrow box Ford Flareside was still offered, but relatively few were specially ordered.

For 1957 the 110in wheelbase F-100 received an all-new look that was a complete contrast to GM's softer, more rounded styling, in both its cars and trucks. Engines offered included the slightly more powerful 139hp, 223ci Six, and the 171hp, 272ci Y-block V8. Power brakes and the Fordomatic transmission were popular options. Today, the collector truck world greatly favors GM's styling over the angular Fords. The Canadian Mercury versions from 1957-60 had a very different front end appearance, with a unique hood, grille, and quad headlight design. (N Mort Collection)

Pictured in this 1958 brochure is a Ford F-100 Styleside pickup with a 6½ft, all-steel box with a 56ft³ capacity. Just visible in the background is a Flareside with an advertised extra-strong wooden floor. (N Mort Collection)

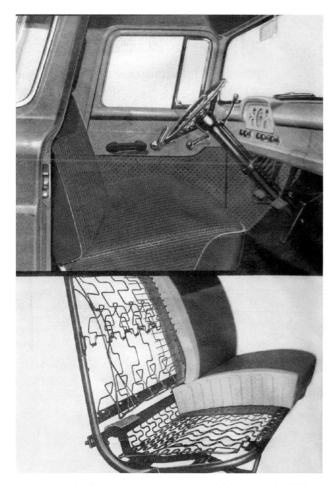

For 1958 Ford offered two basic engines in its F-100 ½-ton pickups. The 139hp, 223ci Six with 208lb-ft of torque @ 2000-2600rpm was standard equipment. The optional 181hp, 272hp V8 came with 283lb-ft of torque @ 2200-2700rpm. (N Mort Collection)

The tailgate opening was wider, at 50.5in, on the steel-floored, reinforced 6ft or 8ft box. The runningboard and full fender Flareside retained its wooden floor and steel skid strips.

The smooth, modern styling of the new Ford pickup trucks was further enhanced by such changes as a 3½in lower overall height, a flat hood, slab-sides and inboard steps concealed by the doors. Only the front grille and headlamp design were similar to the 1956 model. Offered again were two-tone paint schemes – a total of eight – with Colonial White on the upper half.

Back, too, was the safety designed deep-dish steering wheel, and optional 'panoramic' rear window. Other new safety features included standard 'Double-Grip' door locks, a rearview mirror, plus an optional padded dash and seatbelts.

Inside, a new dash design included a cigarette lighter, a larger, more adjustable, comfortable and

A comfortable cab was promised – and delivered – in 1958, and featured non-sag, formed wire springs in the full bench seat. There was also 4in of foam on the seat, and 2in in the seatback. The seat was covered in free-breathing, woven plastic seat upholstery, which was claimed to be cooler in the summer, longer wearing, and easy to clean. (N Mort Collection)

For the 1959 Ford pickups, apart from the grid-style grille being replaced by horizontal bars, the only other changes were in the appearance of the parking lights, and a reshaped hood. Also, in 1959, for the first time, Ford offered its own factory-built 4x4 pickups (for years Marmon-Herrington conversions had been offered). The slogan for Ford trucks in 1959 was 'Go Ford-ward!'
(N Mort Collection)

colorful bench seat, two sun visors, an overall quieter cab and the introduction of suspended floor pedals.

For 1958, Ford's F-100 stylists performed the annual badge, grille and headlight redesign. A grid-style grille was fitted, and for the first time dual headlamps. Part way through the production year, the 272ci V8 was replaced by a larger 292ci version.

As the decade closed, only a few changes were made on the F-100 in 1959.

Ford's daring Ranchero

The last half of the 1950s was a decade of great innovation and experimentation for Ford. In an attempt to create undiscovered markets, the company introduced all-new models, ranges and innovations. This niche-marketing approach could be seen in Ford's Thunderbird, its Skyliner retractable hardtop convertible and Sunliner hardtops, the new Edsel, and the ½-ton Ranchero pickup truck.

Opposite: The first generation, full-size Ford Ranchero designs lent themselves well to two- and three-tone paint schemes. The 1957 first year Ranchero models were clean, handsome designs with single headlamps, and a lighter front grille, bumper and trim treatment. In part, the high styling was thanks to a new stamping process, but would eventually suffer from a variety of problems – particularly rust. Both the Ford and a Meteor Ranchero were also built in Canada, but demand proved far less than expected. This was despite attempts to keep the price lower by offering two trim levels and fewer options. The Meteor was offered in base form, as well as the Meteor Custom Ranchero. (Courtesy Country Classic Cars)

In hindsight, the Ranchero was not that new an idea. Hudson had built its car-like truck, and in Australia the highly successful Ute was car-based. In fact, Ford's first pickup trucks had been based on car frames dating back to before the Model T.

Like its Edsel, that debuted the following year, Ford had high expectations and optimism for its new Ranchero ½-ton, introduced on November 12, 1956.

The new 1957 Ranchero provided businessmen with the comfort of a car and the convenience of a truck when hauling was required. It was a sophisticated, stylish way to tow your boat, trailer or racing car. It was also a handsome vehicle to be parked in your driveway in the suburbs.

From an engineering standpoint, although based on Ford's full-size cars, it was the first pickup truck to be fitted with a ball joint and coil front suspension for a car-like ride and easier handling.

The Ranchero was also the first ½-ton pickup to have 'Select-Air' in-dash air-conditioning, although the under-dash 'PolarAire' unit was offered, as was the 'MagicAire' heater and defroster.

The Ranchero came with 223ci six-cylinder power, or a choice of three V8s including the 272ci, 292ci or even a 312ci V8 if desired. Engine access was via an interior release pull for the front-hinged hood to open.

The Ranchero rode on the shorter 116in wheelbase and shared the all-new, more sculptured front end styling of Ford's cars. The side and rear end styling cues, taillights and panel lines mimicked the car line as well. The rear tailgate was dramatically angled. There was lots of chrome trim and body-colored molding on the top edges of the bed and around the cab.

The rear chrome bumper was borrowed from the station wagon, as was the new contoured frame with thicker, stronger and further set apart siderails, which provide not only lower seating, but better occupant protection.

The Ranchero had a payload of up to 1190lb, with a maximum GVW of 4600lb. The rear bed was 6ft long, but with the tailgate down was 8ft. The Ranchero bed floor actually sat atop a Ranch Wagon (station wagon) floorpan.

A wide range of options were offered on the Ranchero, such as power steering, power brakes, a power seat and power windows.

For 1958 Ford's 'Personal' car, the new four-seat Thunderbird, grew to full size, and its quad front lights added luxury. High style was also seen in the fresh-look Ranchero. While the standard Ranchero was nicely equipped, it was the 'Custom' series that came fitted with upgraded interiors, standard passenger armrest and sunvisor, gold inserts in the side moldings, additional polished trim, gunsight ornaments on the tops of the front fenders, and two-tone paintwork.

The engine line-up included the standard 223ci

In 1958 the Ranchero was once again advertised as looking, riding and handling like a car, yet able to work like a truck.
It continued to be shown in truck brochures, and also had its own Ranchero brochure. Despite its car-like appearance, the
Ranchero was never promoted in car literature or advertising. Yet, the Ranchero was a pickup truck for the white collar worker,
or those who hauled on a 'light' or occasional basis. Strangely, the Canadian Ranchero models could not be ordered with optional
A/C, the Signal-Seeking radio or power windows. (Andrew Mort)

six and a wide range of V8s. New was the 300hp, 352ci Interceptor and an available, although unlisted, 332ci V8 in either 240hp or 265hp guise. Four different transmissions were offered.

In 1959 Ford offered only a 118in wheelbase on all its cars, including the Ranchero pickup which gave it a 2in increase and also translated into a bigger rear box on the now single, mildly restyled model 'Custom.' All Ranchero production had been moved stateside for 1959.

Despite a cleaner grille and bumper design and dual headlamps, a mere 52 Meteor Ranchero trucks were built in 1958, of which 38 were six-cylinder models, before all Ranchero production moved stateside. Dual headlamps were legal as of 1958 in all 48 US states, and in Canada's ten provinces. As well as improved lighting, the dual headlamps provided stylists with a means of incorporating a fresh, new look. (Andrew Mort)

The restyled hood, grille, parking lights and bumper were conservative, considering the new El Camino competition, but buyers bought more Fords than dramatic bat-wing Chevs. Once again the side molding was changed, and this year the tail lights and tailgate were, too. Inside, the dash and instrumentation was changed. Ford sold 14,169 Rancheros in 1959. In Canada reportedly only 558 Ford Ranchero trucks were built in Oakville in the short 1957 production run, but the lack of interest continued in 1958 with just 86 constructed. As a result, all Ranchero production shifted to the US in 1959.
(N Mort Collection)

Meteor Ranchero

Ford of Canada, with its different Mercury and Meteor line-up, was quick to add a Meteor Ranchero later in 1957. Like all the other unique-to-Canada Mercury and Meteor truck models, they were distinctive in trim, colors, optional equipment, front and rear end styling.

Mechanically, both Division's trucks were identical, other than the Meteor's transmission being referred to as the Merc-O-Matic.

The biggest visual differences were the distinctive Meteor grille that was lifted-off the sedan range, and the distinctive two-tone color paint combinations.

Just 300 Meteor Ranchero trucks were constructed in the 1957 model run. There were even fewer being built the following year, and thus the decision was made to halt 1958 Canadian Ranchero production after just two months.

Ford and the Canadian Mercury ½-ton pickup trucks

Following WWII, Ford resumed production of its prewar ½-ton truck designs, and the first Canadian-built Mercury truck appeared in 1946-1947, following the restructuring of Ford of Canada. It was designated the M47, which stood for its 4700lb GVW.

Whereas Ford of Canada and Ford-Monarch dealers were retailing Ford trucks, it would be the Lincoln-Mercury-Meteor showrooms that carried the Mercury truck line, which also included a Meteor sedan delivery. One often noted, practical reason for offering Mercury trucks in Canada was the fact that many of the

In 1952, the Mercury front end styling and trim was seen on the full line of Mercury trucks. The interiors also shared the same styling cues, layout and materials.
(N Mort Collection)

smaller communities in the Provinces had only one Ford Motor Company outlet, which was either a Ford or a Mercury dealership. Although true, so was the fact that automakers had a long history of offering unique models in Canada, which had loyal buyers. Mercury trucks would not be offered in the United States, but would be sold throughout the commonwealth.

The Ford and Mercury pickups were almost identical, but each make had its own distinctive chromed grille, badges, script, bumpers, and headlamp and tail lamp bezels. The Mercury was noted for its fancier exterior. Particularly unique on the Mercury cab was an optional sliding rear window. Also, the interiors were generally

better dressed with a bit more brightwork and trim, either standard or offered as an option by the factory.

The engines offered in the Mercury truck line were the same as those available in the Ford models.

In 1948, when the all-new Ford 'Bonus Built' pickup trucks appeared, Mercury once again had its upmarket, slightly different-looking equivalent. In fact, Mercury also offered its own version of every other Ford truck available.

Throughout the 1950s there would be less of a difference in the overall appearance between the Ford and Mercury truck models, other than badging, minor fittings, and the rear tailgate stampings.

Along with the ½-ton Mercury pickup, there were 79 other Mercury truck models in the line-up by 1952.

Ford of Canada ceaed all Mercury truck production in 1968. At that time, it was offering close to 280 different Mercury truck models.

There was little to differentiate this 1952 Mercury M1 pickup from the previous year, other than minor chrome trim changes. The 1952 Ford and Mercury models were replaced in March 1953 with fresh, more modern-looking front end styling. (N Mort Collection)

Stylish Chevrolet and GMC

Chevy was quick off the mark after WWII, with a freshly styled 'Advance-Design' pickup truck that began production on May 1, 1947. The fender-mounted lights and vertical chrome grilles had gone, and the clean 'Unisteel' cab styling now consisted of a grille with a series of five long horizontal bars spanning almost the entire front end, and rectangular running lights. The large rounded fenders came with flattened sides for a somewhat taller, trimmer look.

In 1950, the 5-window cab option of Chevrolet's ½-ton pickup was available as a Series 3100. Despite providing better all-round vision in an era of optional rear view mirrors, it was more expensive, and thus not as popular for farm, maintenance and construction work. (N Mort Collection)

By 1950, pickup truck owners were demanding more dress-up, as well as functional extras on their pickup trucks. Driving lights and foglamps were common aftermarket additions, as were two rearview mirrors, and exterior sun visors. Aftermarket exterior sun visors were originally made of steel, but later were molded fiberglass. These sun visors were also fitted on cars in the 1940s and '50s, and continued to be popular with pickup truck owners right into the 1980s. This two-tone 1950 Chevrolet 1300 is a fine example of a restored, shortbox Stepside, powered by its original 235ci six-cylinder engine. (N Mort Collection)

Proportionately, the Advance-Design trucks weren't the sleekest machines, but were still considered stylish and contemporary in their day.

Chevrolet had beaten Ford in total truck production for the first time in 1939, and it was determined to be number one. For the next three decades Chevrolet held this honor, although it depended on whether it was based on the calendar year or model year in some cases.

By 1950, the three year old Advanced-Design required some refreshing. Although only minimal changes were made to the exterior, inside, a wider, more comfortably sprung seat could be found, and the overall ride improved, thanks to the dropping of the lever shocks in favor of the double-acting shock absorbers, first seen on the car line in 1949.

In its fifth year Chevrolet continued to make minor changes to keep its 3100-Series light pickups competitive. Vent panes were added to the side doors and the rearview mirror was lowered. The seat cushion was further refined for improved comfort.

Mechanically there were numerous positive changes. The front and rear brakes were redesigned, providing smoother, more effortless braking.

This 1951 Chevrolet ½-ton survivor now has a most unusual stance, as the body has been mounted on a 1988, four-wheel-drive GMC chassis, for current farm use. (N Mort Collection)

Durability was enhanced by making available two additional heavy-duty generators, longer-lasting brake facings and better seals.

Although more expensive than a Ford F-100, the 1951 3100-Series offered more standard features and more options. Features such as standard 2-speed wipers, a cab ventilator on the left side, a chrome bumper, a hold-open door device, and a stronger tailgate were appreciated by operators. Options such as a chrome grille and a chrome windshield and bright window moldings provided a dressier look.

For 1952 the once standard back bumper was now an option, which resulted in tucking-in the rear taillights, spare tire, license plate and tailpipe for better protection.

After peaking at 441,281 units in 1950 (which included ¾-ton, 1-ton, stake, panel, canopy and Carry-All Suburban models) sales declined to a low of 290,953 light-duty trucks in 1952, but rebounded to 327,546 trucks in 1953. Although these were all healthy production figures, it means this 1952 Chevrolet 1300 ½-ton is just a little rarer today.
(N Mort Collection)

In 1953 General Motors of Canada was building this Chevrolet 1314 in its Oshawa, Ontario plant. This restored example was one of 8803 pickups built there that year. The light blue 1308 Series pickup was powered by a 105hp, 235ci, inline six-cylinder engine, with a 3-speed manual transmission as a column shift, offered for the first time by Chevy and GMC. It was carefully restored to original condition, and the factory colors matched. (N Mort Collection)

And without the rear bumper, the tailgate could be dropped straight down for easier loading. A new option was a spotlight, while the grille guard accessory was redesigned to be stronger, lower, and wider, and thus provide greater protection.

Now in its seventh year, the design required further changes to remain competitive, and accommodate new state laws coming into effect for 1953. For the first time, factory turn signals were fitted to meet safety regulations made mandatory in some states. Other improvements found inside included a larger steering wheel, a restyled dash, and new colors and upholstery fabrics.

From the outside a redesigned hood badge provided a telltale sign that the 3100 was a 1953 model. The standard green color was now Juniper, but other colors were available at no extra cost. A rear bumper and left-side mounted spare were optional, as was tinted glass.

The 1954 Chevrolet and GMC pickup trucks were unique in that two series were offered that differed considerably in appearance. While the first series appeared with just minor styling changes, the second series sported a wrap-around windscreen, which resulted in a change in both the Cab's A-pillars and side glass.

GM became the leader in the new trend for greater style in pickups when it introduced its second, all-new pickup truck models since WWII.

Like its Chevrolet sibling, the GMC ½-ton pickup truck was also sold in 1954 in two different Series. This is the later, more modern Series featuring a redesigned cab with its one-piece curved windscreen, a redesigned dash and new steering wheel. Note the optional radio, chrome grille and overriders fitted. The second series 1954 Chev and GMC pickups were given an increase in power. The perennial 228 six-cylinder engine was out, in favor of the more powerful, larger 125hp, 248ci Six. (N Mort Collection)

For 1955 Chevrolet introduced its ultra-stylish Cameo Carrier and GMC-equivalent Suburban. These models were fitted with all the deluxe options and equipment. The unique 'Speed-Line' styling consisted of additional fiberglass outer panels, which ran the length of the body, and flowed into a different bumper and tailgate design. The Cameo Carrier was the inspiration for the entire Fleetside line introduced in 1958. Pictured is the 1956 Chevrolet Cameo Carrier model. (N Mort Collection)

In the spring of 1955 Chevrolet and GMC introduced their virtually all-new trucks, both sharing their own individual, tasteful front end styling throughout their respective, entire line-ups.

The old truck styling had dated back to 1947, while this 'Speed-Line Styling' took its inspiration from the 1955 Chevrolet 'Motoramic' show car line-up.

The single unit design of the cab was very unique in its day. The upper greenhouse with its wrap-around windscreen featured forward leaning A-pillars. The cab roof design was called, 'military school cadet peak cap.' The rear window was also a wrap-around style, making for an extraordinarily slim B-pillar. The cab doors were deep and concealed a large inner step for ease of entry.

On the Chevy, the new single unit, front end featured a trapezoidal grille sitting below a 3-D chrome winged badge on the hood. The front fenders featured hooded, inset headlamps with flat-tops and flared edge wheelwell openings. A nicely defined side crease ran from just behind the headlight, through the door and onto the rear flared fender.

GMC put its own individual spin on the front end styling with similarly, tasteful results.

A new addition to the line-up was the Chevrolet Model 3204, and its GMC equivalent, which comprised a ½-ton built on a ¾-ton chassis, with a longer box for bulky, but not necessarily heavy loads. Also, a premium Chevrolet Cameo and GMC Suburban (first called the Town and Country), joined the ½-ton line-up. The GMC version had its own front end styling, V8 powerplant, and unique dash layout.

Under the hoods of the new pickups were big changes too. For 1955, Chevrolet pickups could be powered by an OHV 145hp, 265ci Trademaster V8. The standard engine for all 3000-Series trucks was the 123hp, 235ci Thriftmaster six.

GMC chose to go with the 155hp, 288ci recalibrated version of the Pontiac V8, while minor modifications were made to the GMC 248ci six-cylinder engine.

The new truck frames incorporated the 34in side rail spacing, as recommended by the Society of Automotive Engineers (SAE), along with improvements in steering, braking and the rear end.

The 1955 GMC styling was dubbed 'Blue Chip,' while the fresh Chevrolet trucks were known as 'Task Force.'

The stylish Task-Force pickups helped Chevrolet

Chevrolet ½-ton Pickup Truck

The new 1955 Task Force Chevrolet and GMC Blue Chip pickup trucks were considered by many to be as handsome in appearance as Chevrolet's cars. The trucks were promoted with the slogan, 'Modern Design for Modern Hauling.' A new 34in-wide parallel frame replaced the old tapered version which no longer conformed to industry standards. A cowl-top grille provided flow-thru ventilation, and, combined with the double-layered insulated cab roof, helped keep the interior cooler. (N Mort Collection)

The 1000in² wrap-around rear window on the Task Force Chevrolet and GMC Blue Chip pickup trucks provided plenty of all-round vision, while a rear chrome bumper and wooden side rails added even more pizazz to this already stylish truck. Deluxe cab options included polished stainless windscreen, cab moldings and trim, vent windows, an expanded two-tone paint scheme, a chrome grille, bumper, and headlamp bezels, full wheel discs, and dual horns. Between the two GM brands were only subtle mechanical, interior, trim and styling differences.
(N Mort Collection)

gain 34.5 percent of the overall truck market and a calendar production total of 329,791 units. 1955 also saw Chevrolet build its six millionth truck, while GMC saw truck production increase to a total of 104,750 units.

There were only minor cosmetic changes for 1956, but the new V8 engines were upgraded. The six-cylinder models now joined the V8s in adapting a 12-volt system, as introduced in 1955. Factory, non-military 4WD pickups were also introduced in 1956.

Chevrolet's V8 saw a power increase to 155hp, while over at GMC, its Pontiac-based V8 was increased to 316.6ci and now rated at 180hp. The standard Chevy

and GMC Six were enlarged to 270ci and capable of producing 130hp.

For 1957 the light-duty truck models from Chevrolet and GMC again received only minor face-lifts and trim changes along with suspension and running gear improvements. Inside, a deep-dish style steering wheel was fitted. The Cameo Carrier and Suburban featured new side decorative treatment, which was trimmed in chrome and painted a contrasting body color. The Cameo Carrier was available in eight contrasting colors. Despite its added glamor, Chevrolet sold only 2572 examples and GMC far fewer of its Suburban sibling.

Chevrolet's 265ci V8 increased in performance to

The Chevrolet version in 1955 featured its own unique dash design dominated by the V-shaped speedometer. Chevrolet also had its own range of options, including unique interior materials and patterns. The redesigned interior featured two-tone vinyl and paint door panels, a vinyl, patterned headliner, and new padded, woven fabric seat upholstery for added comfort and style. (N Mort Collection)

For 1956, the GMC ½-ton was promoted as the worker's truck. One advertisement read: "If you have a stake in America's booming construction program, we 3000 GMC dealers are ready to equip you as no one else can do. In any truck for any purpose – light duties to heavy – there's a great GMC waiting for you!" (N Mort Collection)

162hp, yet GMC once again followed Pontiac Division's lead, which saw its V8 engine increased to 347ci, and resulted in a best in the industry pickup power rating of 206hp. The standard six-cylinder received a power boost to 140hp.

In 1958, similar styling cues were seen on GM's entire line-up, including its much larger GMC and Chevy trucks. In February 1958, and standard for the first time on GM's ½-ton and ¾-ton pickup trucks, was a full width 6½ft or 8ft smooth-sided box. These pickups became known as the Chevrolet Fleetside and GMC Wide-Side. Gone was the Cameo Courier, with just 375 units

The restyled '57 Chevy ½-tons received a redesigned hood and grille, plus different trim, badges and script to set them apart from their predecessors. In 1957 Chevrolet was once again the largest manufacturer of trucks in America, building 351,739 units and capturing 32.4 percent of the market as a result. (Andrew Mort)

having been sold, along with a trickle of GMC Suburban versions.

Chevrolet's optional V8 was now the 283ci Trademaster which replaced the old 265ci motor, while the six-cylinder engine with increased compression was rated at 140hp.

Although Pontiac was again upgrading its V8, GMC decided to do things differently and went with a smaller

The 1957 Chevrolet truck line-up was given a corporate face-lift. The new grille now consisted of double trapezoidal inserts; painted, as was the bumper on the standard cabs. (Andrew Mort)

Both the new double trapezoidal grille inserts and the bumper were chrome on the Deluxe versions, as seen here. (Andrew Mort)

The 3100-Series ½-tons were built on a 114in wheelbase, while the 3200-Series rode on a 122.25in wheelbase. (Andrew Mort)

This rare 1957 Chevrolet Cameo Carrier is even more unique than usual, due to the fact it is an all-original, unrestored example. Despite the Cameo Carrier's ever-increasing value, this ½-ton is still doing yeoman tasks on a daily basis. First introduced in 1955, these models were responsible for heralding in the new change in pickup truck philosophy. (Courtesy Bill Peeters)

Dual headlamps were all the rage in 1958, and few looked better than those on this Canadian Chevrolet Apache Series 31. For 1958 Chevrolet changed not only its number designations, but also applied names to its truck lines, with Apache for its light-duty, Viking for its medium-duty and Spartan for its heavy-duty models. There were the usual minor changes to the grille design and trim, but dual headlamps provided an even fresher look. (N Mort Collection)

bore, which resulted in a slightly less powerful 200hp, 336.1ci V8.

For 1958 GMC also introduced its new Wide-Side pickups with dual headlamps and restyled front fenders, hood and grille which carried the Series number. A more elaborate side trim was also applied.

The GMC pickup truck's styling actually had more than a hint of '56 Cadillac in its lines. These Wide-Side models went on to replace the Suburban late in the year.

The Series 100, Model 101-8, ½-ton pickup was known amongst pickup truck owners for having the best power-to-weight ratio.

American actor Steve McQueen owned a Series 100, Model 101-8, ½-ton. The 1958 GMC pickup was one of McQueen's favorites out of his many motorcycles, sports cars and other vehicles. The truck was housed with his collection kept at the Beverley Wiltshire hotel during the time he lived there. This pickup was once described by the late actor's wife Barbara as "Steve's baby."

Overall in the industry, 1958 was not a good year. Production levels industry-wide dropped to 1945 levels – including trucks – and GMC recorded its lowest production numbers in nearly two decades.

In 1959, as the decade came to an end, the Chevrolet and GMC ½-ton pickups on the outside

The new 31 (3100) or 32 (3200) 1959 ½-ton pickups were virtually identical in styling and trim to the '58 models, other than a new grille and changes in molding trim. The ½-ton 3200 Stepside was built on the longer wheelbase, ¾-ton chassis, and fitted with a 'Long Bed' or 'Long Box.' Despite this, these pickups were rated with the same 5000lb GVW maximum in 1959. (N Mort Collection)

GM's Chevrolet alone offered a total of 139 different Task-Force truck models in 1959, including the ½-ton Fleetside and Stepside pickups, as well as an all-new Chevrolet El Camino. (N Mort Collection)

In 1959 Chevrolet took its new station wagon and basically removed its roof from the B-pillar back above the belt line. The styling result was very dramatic with the new 1959 Bat-Wing design. The rear cargo area was double-lined, over 6ft long, almost 5½ft wide, had a volume of 34ft^3 and reportedly could haul a maximum of 1150lb. The tailgate lowered to the bed floor level for carrying extended loads. The maximum GVW was 4900lb for the 119in wheelbase El Camino. Apart from the standard Six, two optional V8s were offered. A 3-speed manual could be replaced by a Powerglide, Turboglide, or overdrive transmission. (N Mort Collection)

remained virtually the same, with badge changes, a different trim line, two-toning on the Fleetside and Wide-Side, and a reduction in the size of the restyled front bumperettes. The interiors also received minor styling revisions.

A redesigned camshaft in the Six provided 10 percent better mileage, and Chevrolet's optional V8 was a 140hp, 283ci.

The GMC/Pontiac V8 underwent more changes to its crankshaft and bore, but retained its 336ci displacement and previous horsepower rating.

Sales bounced back for both Chevrolet and GMC, and promised even brighter days ahead with 'Operation High Fear' set in motion for the sixties.

Chevrolet's El Camino – the new pickup in town!

Replacing the high-styled Cameo Carrier in 1959 was the all-new El Camino. (GMC didn't get its own version, but the Suburban name survived and was reapplied in its model line-up.)

The El Camino was based on Chevrolet's full-size car line and featured a double-lined, strengthened floor with added cross-members, and a rear box with ½-ton hauling capacity. Ironically, due to the El Camino's car-based origins, it had a great stance when unloaded, but hauling a heavy load gave it a nose-high look, and didn't help handling. Optional heavy-duty springs resolved that problem, but when the box was empty the rear

Described in its advertising, as, "More than a car … More than a truck," the new El Camino was the first Chevrolet coupe pickup since the 1941 production coupe could be ordered with an optional box fitted into the trunk. It was the answer to Ford's equally stylish and very similar Ranchero which had first appeared in 1957. (Earlier similar 1936 coupe/pickup version pictured.) (Andrew Mort)

end provided the El Camino with an unorthodox, raked look.

The base model 1180 was powered by the 135hp, 235ci six-cylinder engine and the model 1280 by a V8. There were four versions of the 283ci V8 to choose from including an 185hp or 230hp carbureted version, or a 250hp or 290hp fuel-injected version. There were five other 348ci V8s to choose from too: a four-barrel rated at 250hp, a three two-barrel version pumping out 280hp, a four-barrel at 305hp and two choices of three, two-barrel V8s rated at 315hp and 335hp.

In the American magazine *Hot Rod* in 1959, testers recorded a quarter mile speed of 90mph and a 0-60mph time of 8.7 seconds for the 315hp, 3880lb El Camino.

The base sticker price for the El Camino was US$2740, but like the Ranchero, sales for the El Camino fell short of expectations with a total of just 22,246 units. The new decade would force Chevrolet to rethink its future for the El Camino.

Still number one in trucks, the Chevrolet Division was not about to let Ford own this market niche. On the El Camino most of the trim, chrome fittings, and rear window were borrowed from the Chevrolet Bel Air. The basic interior fittings came from the full-size, least expensive, Biscayne model. Options such as air-conditioning and power windows gave the El Camino a touch of class. Also, to accentuate its high-flying style, the El Camino could be ordered in 13 solid colors, or ten two-tone paint jobs. (N Mort Collection)

Dodge and Fargo

'Straight out of tomorrow'

Dodge and Fargo

The Dodge brothers began building trucks in Detroit in 1916, and their company prospered, but shortly after the brothers died, the firm was purchased by empire builder Walter P Chrysler. In 1927 it became the Dodge Division of the then three-year-old Chrysler Corporation.

Fargo trucks were introduced by Chrysler in 1928 as its Fleet Sales organization, and used in Canada as well as for Canadian exports around the world. Fargo models were identical to Dodge trucks except for nameplates and different cosmetic trim, and were not sold in the United States.

Dodge and Fargo trucks had a solid reputation for reliability throughout the 1930s and '40s, and the two divisions built over 500,000 military trucks from 1943-1945. In 1947 Dodge had a record truck-building year, but fresh designs were introduced in 1948, including its all-new B-Series ½-ton pickup. Dodge's familiar 'Job-Rated' slogan was once again used in promotions.

Dodge and Fargo in the 1950s were very much like Ford and Mercury, and GMC and Chevrolet, in that they differed only slightly in model line-up, nameplates, trim and options, or, in the case of Mercury and Fargo, were often sold in specific countries and markets only.

By 1950 the B-Series was already in its third year of production, and in the two previous years there had been no changes whatsoever. Still, apart from a few mechanical and layout improvements, it remained virtually the same. The ½-ton was offered on a 108in wheelbase with a 6½ft box. A 95hp, 217.8 L-head straight Six was the only engine offered.

In 1951 strict material controls had been put in place by the National Production Authority (NPA) for defense production, yet it was a truck industry record year. By the third quarter of 1951, materials were allotted on a percentage basis, according to the individual truck manufacturer's civilian market share. The estimate was based on production from 1947 to 1949. Dodge went on to break an all-time production record for its trucks with 188,690 units built: a production total that wouldn't be broken until 1968.

In February 1951, a refreshed B-Series was unveiled.

In the 1930s and '40s, Dodge and Fargo had a good reputation for reliability, and, between them, built over 500,000 military trucks from 1943-45. The all-new B-Series ½-ton pickup was a fresh new design for 1948, after a record truck-building year in 1947.
(N Mort Collection)

The face-lift provided a slightly more attractive-looking front end and an all-round beefier look. A chrome 'Job-Rated' badge was placed between the two grille bars and the new hood was lower. Power was increased to 95hp, while inside there were numerous improvements:

The 1951 Fargo ½-ton pickup was promoted on its added standard features, which included 'Fluid Drive,' a larger capacity fuel pump, an improved ignition and electrical system, easier loading (thanks to a lower ground-to-floor height) and easier handling through the addition of new worm-and-roller steering gears. (N Mort Collection)

changes included a redesigned instrument panel with the instruments now positioned in front of the driver, and the addition of cardboard trim panels.

Fluid-Drive proved to be popular, and as a result Dodge dealers noted more and more women were buying and driving 'family' trucks. A popular option was the choice of a high-sided box over the standard low-side version for greater load capacity.

The NPA controls continued into 1952 due to the Korean 'Police Action.'

Apart from the specific model code being changed from B-2-B to B-3-B, the 1952 Dodge ½-ton trucks were identical in appearance and mechanical specifications. The only identifying change was the 'Job-Rated' grille medallion, which was now painted silver, due more to the ongoing 'Korean Conflict,' as it was referred to, rather than a war.

For 1953 a new chrome and painted, block letter badge on the hood, chrome headlamp and parking bezels, and reshaped, more streamline rear fenders provided a new look. An industry first option (US$13.28) was the new, longer 7½ft high-side bed which was a ½-ton pickup built on a ¾-ton 116in wheelbase.

Inside, the interiors were upgraded with new color combinations. Options included an automatic 'Truck-O-Matic' transmission and the six-cylinder engine upgraded to 100hp. A two-tone 'Spring Special' in 1953 was announced to help boost sagging sales.

Although it was time for an all-new ½-ton pickup truck from Dodge, the disastrous sales showing in 1953 wasn't due so much to Ford's new pickup design, but rather more because of the fierce sales competition between Ford and Chevrolet which saw drastic price-cutting to achieve sales.

Thus, with an all-new 1954 C-1-Series cab and

frame design, hopes were high for an increase in market share.

The overall styling was familiar Dodge, but the new curved windscreen, trapezoidal grille with different sized parallel bars sporting chrome trim panels in the center, and reshaped hood, provided a thoroughly updated appearance.

The cab could be dressed in a choice of three

Surprisingly, extensive changes were made to the now-designated 1953 B-4-B in its final two years of production, but the new options, fresh interior and exterior styling failed to attract buyers. (N Mort Collection)

There were few changes for 1954 on either the Dodge or Fargo, and there was nothing very fancy about the example pictured. This advertisement stressed only the practical features of saving loading time, delivery time, and low maintenance costs. (N Mort Collection)

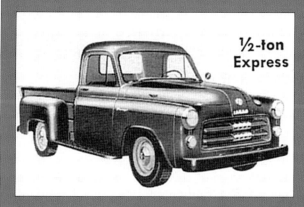

Even the 1954 literature was a carry-over until the spring of '55 when the new C-3 models were introduced. Standard engine was the 110hp, 230ci L-Head Six at a sale price of $1339.25. Pictured is a 1955 C-3B with a low-side box. (N Mort Collection)

two-tone trim levels: Standard, Deluxe and Custom. Egress and ingress were easier thanks to a lower sitting cab. Visibility was improved with the standard, larger greenhouse and could be improved further by adding the optional rear corner cab windows.

At first only the standard six-cylinder was offered, but by August 1954 the new 241ci Hemi V8 was available in the ½-ton, and a soon-to-come new 110hp, 230ci L-head Six was also announced. The new OHV Power Dome V8 gave Dodge the title of 'The Most Powerful Pickup,' and the Division proved that fact at Pike's Peak and the Bonneville Salt Flats, almost equalling some of the best runs by the top stock cars.

As 1954 drew to a close, truck sales were beginning to increase for Dodge and continued to do so in 1955. There had been no changes to the 1955 C-1-Series pickups for most of the year – there was no designated C-2 – but on April 11, 1955, the new C-3-Series was announced.

A lot of the credit for the phenomenal increase in sales in 1955, though, has to go to Dodge's new Hemi V8, along with the offering of the Division's first fully automatic, two-speed, column-shift 'Powerflite' transmission.

1955 was also the first year Dodge offered an overdrive transmission, plus the fact that tubeless tires were now standard on the ½-ton pickup trucks. Prices started at US$1501 for a ½-ton in 1955, but sale prices were promoted to encourage sales. The manufacturer's suggested retail price would officially increase by US$29.00 for the new 1956 C-3 models.

In 1956 Dodge large truck sales increased 27 percent, but light truck sales and overall corporate profits at Chrysler slumped again in the US. In comparison, Canadian sales increased, and were the

The retail price for the 1955 ½-ton Dodge C-3B Job-Rated pickup started at US$1501. In 1956 the window sticker base price would rise by $29.00 for the newest version of the C-3 models. The top-of-the-line pickup was known as the Custom Regal, and sold for US$1645 when equipped with the standard six-cylinder engine. For V8 power the customer needed to pay an additional $120.00.
(N Mort Collection)

second highest ever. Chrysler's overall market share was up by almost 1 percent to 23.8 percent of the total market.

Apart from sheet metal changes, the 1957 through 1960 Dodge trucks remained the same. Yet Dodge trucks excelled due to the styling genius of Virgil Exner. Exner had taken over styling in 1955 and by '57 had incorporated his 'Forward Look' which was described as being 'straight out of tomorrow.'

New for 1957 was the 'Forward Look' of the car line-up on all Dodge pickups. Stylist Exner had to contend with existing basic designs, and so the changes were limited to reforming the sheet metal. The front fender lines were extended forward and the headlamps became hooded. The entire front end was remodeled for a fresh appearance including new grille treatments and a different bumper. The hood opened 45 degrees, or full 90 degrees for easy engine servicing. The stylists had succeeded in making the Dodge pickups seem as they were in motion even at rest.

While Ford, Chevy and GMC may have been the sales leaders in the pickup truck market in 1957, it was the new Dodge Sweptside that was the style leader.

The 1956 Fargo was virtually identical to its Dodge brethren, other than for a bit of trim and badges. The corporation's 'Forward Look' symbol was now on the sides of the fenders instead of the traditional Fargo script. In Canada, it wasn't until 1957 that the V8 engine was available.
(N Mort Collection)

1956 saw tubeless tires, a 12-volt electrical system, a heftier generator, and sealed beam headlamps fitted as standard equipment. There was also a higher GVW and GCW. The Dodge and Fargo ½-ton pickup trucks could also be ordered with optional power brakes, and a pushbutton 'LoadFlite' automatic transmission. (N Mort Collection)

Dodge Sweptside pickups came standard with the Custom cab, which added a glove box lock, Saron and Rayon seat material covering with foam rubber cushions, two sun visors, a wrap-around rear window, and two-speed wipers. Custom cab exteriors featured additional chrome trim and embellishments. In addition to its stylish derriere, Dodge offered the Sweptside with two-tone paint, wide whitewall tires, and full wheel covers. Optional was a 204hp, 314.6in³ V8 engine, power steering and brakes, and an automatic transmission. The Sweptside's only full year of production would be 1958. (N Mort Collection)

Late in the 1957 model year (May), Dodge introduced its K-Series D100 Sweptside pickup truck, to compete with Chevy's Cameo Carrier and Ford's all-new Ranchero car-based pickup.

The Sweptside D100 featured the flamboyant rear fins, and other styling cues, grafted onto a long box from Dodge's own two-door station wagon. The rear bumper from the wagon was also fitted, along with some quarter moldings for a true swept look.

With a substantial increase in sales and profits for 1958 there were few changes. The Sweptside D100 was seen as the most stylish and one of the most able haulers in the industry, but style had its price. The D100 was priced at US$2124 in 1958. Unfortunately, it was a recession year, and overall truck sales topped-out at a mere 871,330 units, the lowest production total since 1945. Chrysler Corporation's profits sank from $120 million in 1957 to a $34 million loss.

The final year of the decade saw a rebound 30 percent increase in sales resulting in the highest truck industry production total since 1955.

In January of 1959 the good-looking Sweptside was dropped, and an all-new, even more upscale Sweptline was introduced, featuring a cab-wide box. Gone were the fins in favor of a squared-off, flat-sided, plain box.

Changes to the ½-ton pickup truck were limited to a new grille, badges, and script. The big changes would have to wait until the 1960s.

Fargo and DeSoto

The Fargo nameplate was introduced by Chrysler in 1928 as a line of commercial vehicles, but there were some sedans and station wagons to wear that badge. In fact, the corporation stated, "Passenger car lines of the most modern accepted standards are characteristic throughout the Fargo line."

By the 1930 model year, and with sales of just 7680 units, the Fargo Motor Corporation became Chrysler's fleet sales division to introduce into small foreign markets.

Dodge and Fargo trucks were on the whole identical except for badges and trim. A full line-up of Fargo trucks were built in Canada for sale through Chrysler-Plymouth dealers and overseas. Only a small number of Fargo trucks were built in the US, but again, only for export.

Later in the 1960s, the Fargo nameplate was used on some Commer vehicles after Chrysler had assumed control of the British Rootes Group.

In Canada the Fargo nameplate was dropped in 1972, but was continued in Africa, the Middle East, Scandinavia, and elsewhere.

Dodge also built clone DeSoto trucks in the US for export markets starting in 1939. These were sold until that Division of Chrysler was dropped altogether in 1960. At the same time, DeSoto ½-ton pickups were assembled and sold in Brazil, Australia, India, South Africa and Mexico, as well as Turkey, where local production continued past 1960.

Bigger payload

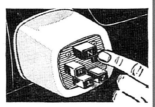

Push-button driving available

Chrysler Corporation offered pushbutton transmissions on in all its cars from the late fifties into the early 1960s. It was thought to be a novel and very modern engineering design, seen as an option on this 1959 Fargo pickup. "Just push the button, and you GO! No clutch to shift, no levers to work." Dodge/Fargo sold 30,758 ½-ton pickup trucks in 1959. (N Mort Collection)

The Fargo Sweptline was a very stylish truck for 1959. It was capable of hauling a payload of up to 3475lb in its 84ft³ of load space. The choice of engines included the powerful 184hp V8 or a more economical 125hp Six. By 1959 the first popular automotive magazines began to test pickup trucks for its readers. (N Mort Collection)

The independents: International, Studebaker and Willys-Overland

International Harvester Company

By 1950, International Harvester had been building light-duty trucks for nearly half a century.

The founders behind International had been Cyrus H McCormick, Henry Weber and William Deering. These three men began their careers in farming equipment and wagons, dating back to the mid-19th century.

Weber established a wagon works, but by the late 1890s it was apparent that the automobile was beginning to challenge the horse. McCormick and Deering had both had a hand at building a horseless carriage, and neither was impressed. In the meantime, the two men merged their respective farming equipment companies along with Weber and two others in 1902, to create 'The International Harvester Company.' Both McCormick and Deering had long associations with farmers, so it wasn't surprising the first International high wheeler 'Autowagon' would debut in 1907.

After the first 100 trucks, a new plant was built in Akron, Ohio, and soon annual production rose to 1000 high wheelers a year. These were produced until 1916.

New truck models were then continually introduced throughout the 1920s, '30s and into the '40s.

International introduced its first ½-ton pickup in

The L-Series trucks were all-new in 1949, and therefore few changes were made in 1950. The front end styling of the new L-Series trucks had seen a dramatic switch from a tall, vertical grille to a short, wide, horizontal design. International followed the industry trend of mounting the headlamps in the front, flat-topped fenders. A slightly curved, one-piece windscreen was thoroughly modern. This L-110 was built and sold in 1950, as can be substantiated by its external door handles, mounted mirrors, and original registration date. (N Mort Collection)

1933, with its Willys-built model D-1. Production began in 1934, but was replaced by International's own C-1 series in 1937.

In the early years of the 1940s, International was the 4th largest builder of light trucks behind Chevrolet, Ford and Dodge, and during the 1950s International was responsible for numerous innovative truck designs both big and small.

The company introduced its now familiar red 'I' over the black 'H' badge in 1944.

The K-Series was introduced in 1941. It quickly became an industry leader and resumed production following the war. Late in 1949 it was replaced by an all-new L-Series with a choice of 87 different models, including a fresh line-up of light-duty trucks.

Launched in January 1950, the new L-Series trucks were a dramatic change in engineering, as well as styling. Production jumped by a third to 26,350 lightweight trucks alone, and helped International record the second highest production total in its history.

The L-Series featured a wider 54½in (48½in between the wheelwells) and 19in deeper box, and, when built on the longer 127in wheelbase, was fitted with an 8ft box. The 115in wheelbase pickups carried a 6½ft box.

Full length runningboards were still incorporated in a rather vertical overall look that was already dated. This was despite being lower, wider, and featuring a horizontal grille. The side-mounted spare tire was set into the rear, left-side fender of the short wheelbase pickups, whereas the longer wheelbase models were mounted on the right ahead of the rear fender.

Unlike the 'Big Three,' International didn't offer a unique line of Canadian models, but there were few Canada-only models, and always minor differences between Canadian-built and American-built L-Series ½-ton pickup trucks. This Canadian-built version bears the distinctive body-colored grille, rather than it being the standard American black. While the early trucks had been referred to as 'Red Babies,' the later 1940s K-Series were known as 'Corn Binders' due to the company's farm connections. This nickname continued on throughout the 1950s. (N Mort Collection)

For the first time International Harvester offered a three-speed column shift in its pickup trucks, such as can be seen in this 1950 L-110 ½-ton. Also, International was quick to point out in its advertising that the L-Series cab was the most spacious in the industry. The dash was well laid out with instrumentation and controls placed directly in front of the driver. The dash was concave, and followed the contour of the curved one-piece windscreen, which was an industry first. (N Mort Collection)

One advantageous feature of the L-Series was its one-piece, curved front windscreen, which was something Ford and the other pickups didn't have until 1953. Interestingly too, the dashboard was also curved. The rear glass was an equally unique two-piece design, and the doors were fitted with vent windows. Inside, the new cab was wider and more spacious.

Bigger news was found under the hood. Gone was the former 214ci, Green Diamond L-Head six. It was replaced by an all-new 220ci, OHV Silver Diamond six-cylinder, with 100hp instead of just 82hp. The new engine sat in a fully redesigned chassis which provided a smoother ride and improved handling.

The L-Series underwent continuous upgrades and minimal styling changes in 1951 and 1952, but it wasn't until January 1953 that substantial improvements resulted in the debut of the R-Series.

The face-lifted R-Series light-duty R-100 and R-110 pickup models were more stylish and less utilitarian in appearance. At the same time it couldn't be considered as more distinctive or glamorous. An increase to 108hp provided a small improvement in performance, and four-wheel-drive was offered as a factory option for the first time.

For 1954 additional models were offered in the light-duty truck range, and an economical 104hp Silver Diamond Six was standard on the short-wheelbase R-100 and R-102 models. Other ½-ton pickup models included the R-110, R-111 and R-112. These were built on both

From 1953 through '55 the International pickups featured this restyled front end, with its more rounded hood and nasal opening, plus the cleaner 'IH' corporate letters on a center horizontal bar. GM's Hydra-matic transmission was an option added in 1955. Although International could tailor a pickup truck for an owner's specific requirements, this made servicing more difficult, as the model designation didn't guarantee it was a standard vehicle. (Courtesy George Kirkham, Southland International Trucks Ltd)

the 115in and 127in wheelbases. With the choice of five different ½-ton models, International could tailor a pickup truck for an owner's specific requirements.

Overall though, there were very few changes, and this could account in part for the average drop in production of over 20 percent for all of International's truck lines.

The last year for the R-Series was 1955. An optional 3-speed, fully automatic transmission was made available late in 1954. A larger, one-piece rear window and deeper side windows, metal inner door panels and tubeless tires were now standard equipment.

The R-100 line rode on 6.70x15 4-ply tires and the R-110, etc models continued to be shoed-in 6.00x16 6-ply tires. Two-tone paint was a new option. All these changes helped overall truck sales jump by over 37 percent.

A substantial redesign took place late in 1955. The new S-Series of 1956 was a designation which hadn't been used since the highly successful 1921-29 model that had established International's reputation as a builder of reputable light trucks.

The interim, short-lived S-Series featured fresher, more contemporary styling, but was still fitted with the L-Series cab. The headlamps were moved into the fenders and separated by a new, wider scooped hood and body-colored grille housing the parking lights.

The hood release was now behind the grille and opened in the more conventional alligator-style. A 12-volt electrical

1956 restyling saw the headlamps return to the fenders, and running lights/turn signals incorporated into the large-mouthed grille. The refreshed front end styling was carried throughout the light-, medium- and heavy-duty model line-up. A new S-100 was priced at US$1662, while the more powerful S-110 cost $1735. Production of the S-Series carried on into early 1957. (Courtesy George Kirkham, Southland International Trucks Ltd)

system was standard in the US (optional in Canada), on this single 115in long-wheelbase ½-ton model. Additional new standard items included a dome light, a fresh-air heater and an oil filter. The more economical S-100 and S-102 models were further de-tuned to 100hp.

The S-Series was gone in 1957, and replaced by the all-new A-Series in celebration of International's 50th 'Golden' anniversary. This Series would take International into the next decade.

The front fenders were restyled providing a forward-

International introduced fresh styling, and another all-new truck line-up for 1957, which included an A-Series Golden Jubilee Anniversary model, fitted with the Custom pickup body, and debuted in the early spring of 1957. These special Anniversary models had all the glitz and glimmer International could think of. In addition, it had all the industry trends such as the smooth-sided box, a wrap-around windscreen, lots of brightwork, and two-tone paint. These celebrated trucks also featured traditional International styling cues of the past, such as a hood scoop, a trapezoidal grille, a tall windscreen, and a bold IH black and chrome badge up-front. (Courtesy George Kirkham, Southland International Trucks Ltd)

thrust, and flatter, more angular look. Gone too, were the dated runningboards and a wrap-around windscreen was fitted. A wider cab and a larger greenhouse made these cabs feel far less claustrophobic.

The standard shortbox pickup went from 6½ to 7ft in 1957, and the 8ft to 8½ft, while the removal of the runningboards provided a more modern look.

International decided to add side steps to assist in the removing of items from the front of the box.

As well as the standard rear-fendered pickup, there was a smooth-sided Custom body offered. This Custom pickup body was only available with a 7½ft box and would be sold just in 1957 and '58. Despite the smooth sides, there was no more room

Golden Jubilee models were fitted with the clean, slab-sided box, and all bore sweeping stainless side moldings, ideal for the model's standard two-tone paint schemes. (Courtesy George Kirkham, Southland International Trucks Ltd)

Late in 1956, International sent out an early press release on a new pickup concept. The six-passenger pickup would be called the Travelette, and was based on the company's existing Travelall station wagon-type hauler, already in production. Two full-width bench seats provided lots of seating for six of either family, farm hands or crew. The price was a hefty $3244 for the B-110 ½-ton. (1959 Travelette pictured.) (N Mort Collection)

The 1957 and 1958 International models came with a standard 12-volt charging system, a redesigned, highly improved cylinder head for the six-cylinder engine, a more colorful, richer, two-tone interior, and better heating and cooling ducting. These were noteworthy improvements over the old cabs. The interior colors offered in Canada were different from those in the US. The Custom pickups with flush rear quarters were fitted with a spring-loaded, one-hand operation tailgate, which was one of the first in the industry. (Courtesy George Kirkham, Southland International Trucks Ltd)

in the box than that of a conventional design with fenders.

Both the Standard ½-ton pickup and the Custom featured side trim and two-tone paint, and the cabs too, were identical in design inside. The tailgate used a latch system making it a one-handed job, and gone were the nasty chains.

A new addition to the line-up in 1957 was the six-passenger cab Model A112 Travelette pickup built on a 129in wheelbase. This crew cab idea was an industry first for International. It was decades before its time, yet largely unappreciated in its day. A 7ft box was fitted to keep the overall length to 210in. The Travelette was offered in both 2WD and 4WD.

The A-Series continued basically unchanged into 1958.

Left: Because the smooth-side Custom pickup body was only available in 1957 and '58 examples are rarely seen today, and is one of the most desirable and sought-after by collectors. The rear fenders were borrowed from the two-door Travelall. More common are the rear external fender variety, such as this one, though still very stylish. Four ½-ton wheelbases were available in 1957, including the 110in, 114in, 126in and 129in (A-series pictured). (Courtesy George Kirkham, Southland International Trucks Ltd)

In 1959, although the face-lift was mild, the addition of standard quad headlamps and a shiny mesh grille as part of a special trim package, went a long way on the new replacement B-Series. The biggest news was the availability of the 266ci V8 across the entire light-duty truck range. A wider box in both 7ft and 8½ft lengths was introduced as the 'Bonus Load.' Unfortunately, the design did not allow items more than 4ft wide to pass through the tailgate.

The overall design of the updated B-Series would carry International's light-trucks through into 1960 with only minimal changes.

They can go *anywhere,*

In 1959 the new rugged International pickup truck line was also available in factory 4x4 guise, as well as offered with a choice of five six-cylinder engines of 220, 240, 264, 282 and 308in³. Or buyers could opt for one of three V8s offered in 260, 304 or 345in³. By the end of the decade, International boasted it had 5000 dealers, 250 factory branches, and 12 parts depots across the US. (N Mort Collection)

The 1959 B100 Bonus-Load Pickup Body featured a box that fitted flush to the cab, to create additional space for cargo. Ease of loading was another feature on the 7 or 8½ft box. Inside, the cab was trimmed and upholstered in durable vinyl. The spacious, wide cab featured a bench seat that was 5ft across. (N Mort Collection)

Studebaker

Studebaker was one of the few independents that went head-to-head with the Big Three when it came to marketing a ½-ton pickup.

By now famous for its new radically-styled, new postwar car designs, Studebaker would also be seen as a ground-breaker when it came to the fresh, modern-looking truck produced at its new factory in South Bend, Indiana. The Chippewa Avenue plant had been previously used by Studebaker during the war, but had been owned by the War Assets Administration. Also, the new pickup truck would be built in Studebaker's Canadian plant in Hamilton, Ontario.

Styling Chief of the Loewy Studio, Bob Bourke, was responsible for the fashionable and advanced design of the new 1949 trucks. (Bourke would continue working with Studebaker, and is credited for the sensational Starliner and Starlight designs that appeared in 1953.)

Studebaker's use of the longstanding 'Coupe Express' designation for its ½-ton was dropped due to it being outdated by 1949, with almost universal adoption by the industry of the term 'pick-up' or 'pickup' truck.

The new 112in wheelbase ½-ton pickup truck was designated the 2R5, and styling was unique compared to Studebaker's car line-up, with only the hubcaps,

1959 International advertising pointed out that the new cab design included a larger windshield with less corner distortion, and no awkward doorway projections, as well as a safer view of the road. There was also a redesigned dashboard with a new, easier to read instrument cluster, and a repositioned accelerator pedal for greater driving comfort. (N Mort Collection)

instrument cluster, steering wheel, some trim parts and headlamp trim rings being borrowed. (Later the Champion model hood ornament would be added to the truck.)

Industry-leading features included a unique, double-lined box, which protected the exterior side panels from load dents and gave the cab and pickup bed a more congruent appearance. A two-tone painted grille kept the costs down by avoiding chrome pieces.

The absence of runningboards (then considered outdated), and a lower ride and loading level added to the 2R5's tasteful appearance. (The 2R5 had a height of 69.75in compared to the previous Studebaker M5-Series 77in and the height of the 1949 Ford F1 pickup at 76.64in.)

The 2R5 with its 6½ft box had an overall length of 185.6in. It could be ordered with or without a box; alternatively fitted with a stake bed; or in a variety of chassis only, cab and partial-cab configurations.

There were few mechanical updates from the previous M-Series, but one notable change was the moving of the non-synchromesh first gear, standard 3-speed shifter from the floor to the steering column. The traditional floor mounted four-speed was optional.

The 2R5 was fitted with the Champion's 80hp, 169.6ci, L-head Six-cylinder engine that was a complete

Styling of the Studebaker 2R5 was by Bob Bourke of the Raymond Loewy Studios, and is considered timeless by many today. Certainly, it was cleaner and more contemporary in 1953 than its rival Chevrolet design. This pickup was the first in America to be specifically designed by a stylist. The new Studebaker pickup truck was designated the 2R as there had been a 1R prototype previously that had been dropped. Throughout 2R5 and 2R6 production from 1949 to 1953, new exterior colors were offered every year. (1950 R2 pictured.) (Courtesy Hyman Motors Ltd Classic Cars)

carryover from the M-Series. Chassis features included an I-beam front axle, a floating rear axle, four-wheel hydraulic brakes, slotted steel wheels and initially lever-arm shocks.

The 2R5 dash instruments, lights, etc were easily accessible from inside the engine compartment via the firewall. There were numerous access hatches in the cab floor for repairs and replacement of the master cylinder or other parts.

The 2R5 boasted such unusual standard equipment as a passenger sunvisor, door armrests, steel interior door panels, panel board kick panels, headliner, rearview and driver's side mirrors, and chrome hubcaps.

All these features, plus excellent visibility and better than average ventilation made the 2R5 an attractive alternative to the comparable Ford or Chevrolet. These pickups would often be pictured in street settings, rather than in traditional work locations. Thus, Studebaker was one of the first manufacturers pushing a pickup truck as an acceptable second or even the only family vehicle for urban living.

Other new Studebaker trucks included a similar looking 2R10 ¾-ton pickup truck with its 8ft box, uprated rear axle and suspension, and the latest 1-ton 2R15 version. There was also a 1½-ton 2R16 and a 2-ton 2R17. Not surprisingly, 1949 would be a record-breaking year for the sale of Studebaker trucks that would never to be equaled again, as truck production reached 67,982 units.

Minimal trim and running gear changes were made in 1950, and, other than the additional exterior colors offered, the pickups were virtually identical in appearance. Although, there were some powerplant

The lack of retooling money was a major factor for the struggling Studebaker, with truck sales slipping from a 1950 total of 52,146 units to 44,714 in 1951. Still, it was tough market competition that had the greatest impact. From a high of 67,981 units in 1948, Studebaker truck sales would continue to decline annually. By 1954 total Studebaker truck sales of all models would tumble to a dismal 12,003 units. (N Mort Collection)

changes in 1950 with the standard six-cylinder receiving a 5hp boost, and later in production a larger engine could be specially ordered. The 102hp, 245.6ci 'Power Plus' Six-cylinder engine was also an option for the 2R6 version of the ½-ton pickup truck. Although few were delivered in 1950, the six did find buyers and would be offered through to 1960.

Studebaker, and the rest of the truck industry, saw production levels slip in 1950 as demand in the civilian truck market softened.

Once again, in 1951 there were few changes made to the 2R5 and 2R6 pickup trucks. An additional 2R6 model was offered, called the 'Trailblazer.' Although it wasn't 4-wheel-drive, it was fitted with smaller, but beefier 900x13 low-pressure tires, designed for driving through sand or snow.

And, although Studebaker introduced a V8 engine in 1951 for its car line-up, this engine was not used in any of its trucks. Yet, the 2R6 with its 'Power Plus' six still had the highest torque compared to all its competitors and was only around 50 dollars more than the 2R5.

Civilian truck production decreased once more due to less demand, and higher prices as a result of the Korean Conflict. Studebaker received a government contract for building 4000 6x6, 2½-ton military trucks, and, as a result, this too cut into its civilian truck production.

For 1952 there were even fewer changes made to the ½-ton pickup truck range, with only the interior accent and trim colors changing.

In its final year in 1953, the Studebaker 2R5 and 2R6 models saw only the addition of the annual new exterior colors and the option of tinted glass. Production of the aging 2R pickup trucks was estimated at just 32,012 units.

Finally in March 1954 the much needed, face-lifted ½-ton models were unveiled with a resulting change in designation to the 3R5 and 3R6.

A modern one-piece, curved windscreen, massive grille that incorporated not only the headlamps, but the turn signal/running lights too, different badging and new smooth hubcaps set the 3R-series apart from its

Following the body drop, power lines are connected and remaining underside bolts tightened from fluorescent-lighted pits running lengthwise down the final assembly line.

Despite being in production for three years, the 1951 2R5 pickup truck had changed very little in styling. Regardless, the basic styling was also the basis of the next generation trucks from Studebaker, and would even be reintroduced in its original form in 1958 and '59 as the low-cost 'Scotsman' model.
(N Mort Collection)

Total production for the 2R5 ½-ton pickup over its 5-year run is estimated at around 110,500, which helped Studebaker, but made little impact in the pickup truck market compared to the average Ford ½-ton pickup production totals, which easily exceeded that annually over the same period. The more powerful 2R6 version reached only 12,500 units. Accurate 2R pickup truck production totals are only available from the Studebaker production plant in Hamilton, Ontario, as in the US, leftover 1949 production models automatically became 1950 models, and so on. Total truck production in Canada never exceeded 1900 units annually. (1952 photo.) (N Mort Collection)

For 1954 Studebaker introduced its face-lifted 3R5 pickup truck, but these styling changes were seen throughout the entire Studebaker truck line-up. Much hope was placed on the newer-look styling, but neither these models, or the subsequent face-lifted generation of pickups of the next decade, would ever equal the sales success of the 2R range. (Courtesy Joseph and Hilda Benincasso)

predecessors. The front bumper was painted the body color and the hood ornament became optional.

Inside was a new dash layout with round instruments, and electrical windscreen wipers became optional. Under the hood was a higher compression version of the six-cylinder, but the new V8 was not offered in the light truck line-up yet. A four-speed transmission was introduced as an option. Despite this, overall truck sales tumbled to an all-time low of just 15,608 units.

For 1955 a name change to the E-Series was tried, and the new E7 ½-ton pickup was available for the first time with the 140hp, 224ci 'Econ-o-miser' V8, and the slightly more powerful 92hp, 185ci 'Econ-o-miser' Six as standard. An automatic transmission was now an option. A minor front end restyling saw a change in the positioning of the parking lights, badge changes, and other minor alterations and additions, to keep up with Detroit's 'annual' model changes. Half-way through the model year Studebaker introduced two-tone paint jobs to enhance its distinctive, but aging styling. Sales increased by about 4000 trucks, but this was a modest increase compared to the competitions' banner year.

The 2E ½-ton pickup trucks underwent yet another name change in 1956, and became known as Transtar to help bring attention to the rather dramatic styling changes. (Ironically, the Transtar name would later be taken-up by International for a truck line.)

The six-cylinder engine(s) were now called 'Work

The smaller V8 was finally dropped in 1957 in favor of the smoother-running, more powerful 170hp, 259ci V8, which became standard in the Transtar ½-ton pickup. Also gone was the four-speed non-synchromesh transmission, replaced by a Borg-Warner all-synchromesh, four-speed. An automatic transmission was optional. Pictured is a 1957 Transtar with a Deluxe cab, powered by the optional 289ci OHV V8 with a Stromberg 2-bbl carburettor and Borg-Warner T-86 Overdrive transmission. This truck was originally delivered to Superior, Arizona, and left the South Bend factory on December 26, 1956. (Courtesy Mark Hayden)

Once again in '57 – despite being very stylish with its two-tone paintwork – those changes with the improved features and mechanical updates had minimal impact. Studebaker's efforts to increase its overall truck market share continued to slip to a total of just 13,642 sales. This fine, restored '57 Transtar's factory options include two-tone paint in Parchment White over Surf Green, which were 1958 Studebaker colors, 2-speed electric wipers, front and rear chrome bumpers, Class B turn signals incorporated with the parking and tail lamps, a 'Climatizer' fresh air heater/defroster unit, and a heavy-duty 40-amp generator. (Courtesy Mark Hayden)

Star,' while the 224ci V8 became the 'Route Star,' and the 259ci V8 was dubbed the 'Power Star.'

Once again the side-to-side front grille was replaced, this time featuring bold vertical bars with a pronounced horizontal frame that flowed into hooded single headlamps and all on the same aging cab. The slightly rounder hood with nacelles provided a bolder, more muscular look, while optional whitewall tires and full wheel discs provided the dressier look that was becoming the market norm. The biggest mechanical improvement for 1956 was the new optional 'Packard Twin Traction' limited-slip differential. Despite the styling

By 1959, despite its simple, but effective front end face-lift and stylish two-toning, the R2-based cab styling of the renamed Transtar, even in Deluxe form, looked dated. An all-new look was needed, but that would have to wait for the next decade. Total Studebaker truck sales in 1959 were just 7737 units. (N Mort Collection)

and feature changes, the new Transtar line failed to attract buyers, and total truck sales for the calendar year slipped to just 15,222 units.

Due to lackluster sales, a bolder, all-new, fiberglass grille, designed by Robert Doehler, and a larger bumper, were introduced on the 1957 pickup trucks. This provided not only a more imposing look, but also one that was more in keeping with the latest seen from the competition. Additional chrome and stylish trim to accentuate the two-toning all helped to freshen-up the nine-year-old design.

Numerous mechanical changes were made, and inside the dash was a simpler, less cluttered design with less moldings, and the ammeter and oil gauges were omitted in favor of warning lights.

The Studebaker Scotsman ½-ton pickup was introduced in 1958 in an effort to boost sales. Unfortunately, 1958 was a recession year in the US with industry truck sales down, which included Studebaker's at just 10,563 total units. (Today considered 'politically incorrect,' the cheap 'Scotsman' notion and resulting nameplate, had already met with moderate success when applied to Studebaker's least expensive car models in 1957.)

With sales still on the decline, Studebaker made a couple of bold moves for 1958. First, it began offering its smaller trucks in factory equipped NAPCO 4x4 guise, including its ½-ton pickup.

Another creative move was to add the 'Scotsman' line of pickup trucks to the dealer's inventory. The Scotsman was advertised as the least expensive ½-ton pickup truck Americans could buy in 1958. The 3E1, powered by the 185ci six-cylinder engine, cost a mere $1595. The Scotsman bore the 1949-53 2R style grille and headlamps. The 'déjà vu' pickup truck had virtually no chrome, and the spare tire was an extra, although the wheel was standard.

Inside there was no padding added to the dash, and the glovebox had no door.

The 1958 Transtar line went essentially unchanged from 1957.

For 1959 the 4E-series was introduced. There were numerous changes in what would be the old pickup's final year. The Scotsman could now be ordered with the 180hp, 259ci V8, had an S badge rather than a decal and got a glovebox door. The Transtar name was dropped in favor of 'Deluxe,' with the biggest visual change being the moving of the parking lights into the fiberglass grille. The Scotsman was powered by the Lark car models' smaller 170ci Six, while the Deluxe V8 was now the larger 210hp or 225hp, 289ci engine. Sales for the year were only marginally higher at 10,779 units.

Over the decade Studebaker management had tried to continually boost its truck sales, and that division had really only survived thanks to an off-and-on flow of US military orders.

In the next decade Studebaker would face even tougher times.

Willys-Overland

Just prior to the war, long established Willys-Overland Motors of Toledo, Ohio was struggling to compete in the new car market, but, following WWII, Willy-Overland continued to build its highly successful military Jeep. The company soon discovered there was a demand for a domestic market Jeep too, and decided to redirect the company toward building only utility vehicles rather than automobiles. Hence, the civilian CJ-2A version was put on sale almost immediately in showrooms across North America.

Then, in 1946 an all-steel 2WD station wagon, also available in 4WD, was marketed, and was quickly followed by a full line of Jeep trucks for 1947.

There were initially a total of 14 body and chassis styles, including a ½-ton pickup truck in 2WD, as well as a 4WD rated at 1-ton. This Willys-Overland line of trucks was designed by well-known stylist Brook Stevens, who incorporated the distinctive Jeep front end in all the models.

The same 63hp four-cylinder engine found in the CJ-2A was fitted, and all the trucks were designed as 4WD and 2WD vehicles to broaden the appeal.

The 2WD Jeep pickup trucks were more expensive than the equivalent Chevrolet and Ford, not to mention more utilitarian-looking. Demand was so high for its 4WD models that production of 2WD pickup trucks ceased early in 1951. The Jeep station wagon and delivery models in 2WD, however, continued in production through to 1965.

Willys-Overland, and subsequently better known as Willys Jeep, Kaiser-Willys and then Kaiser Jeep, was most famous for its 4x4 vehicles, but also offered a pickup truck in 2WD in an attempt to compete in the traditional pickup truck market. Power-wise these trucks were non-contenders, compared to the larger six-cylinder and V8 engines of their rivals. Lack of demand for 4WD was such that 2WD production ceased during 1952. This last of the 2WD line 1952 Willys pickup was ultimately converted to 4-wheel-drive.
(N Mort Collection)

Popular pickup close-ups

1950 Studebaker 2R5

After the highly successful 1949 introduction of its new pickup trucks, Studebaker stayed pat for 1950. Initially only minor changes took place, which included a slight increase in horsepower, minor suspension improvements, and a few trim changes.

A slight increase in compression raised the power of the standard 169.6ci, six-cylinder engine to 85hp, and the maximum torque to 138lb-ft up by 4lb-ft.

When first introduced, Studebaker painted the grilles, front bumper and rear tailgate lettering on all its pickup trucks in 'Tusk Ivory,' but later these were two-toned using the body color. Chrome bumpers were an option. This well restored 1950 2R5 is painted in 'Tuscan Tan.'
(Courtesy Hyman Motors Ltd Classic Cars)

Inside, the new 112in wheelbase 2R pickup trucks had metal door panels, rather than the panel board covers used on the previous M-Series pickup trucks. Yet, the big difference for 1950 was a new horn button – the 1949 design dated back to 1941. Instrumentation consisted of a speedometer, plus amp, fuel, oil pressure and water temperature gauges. (Courtesy Hyman Motors Ltd Classic Cars)

Standard in the 1950 2R5 pickup truck was a slightly more powerful, four main bearing, 85hp, 169.6ci 'Econ-O-Miser' six-cylinder engine, fitted with a Carter one-barrel carburettor. Note optional features fitted. (Courtesy Hyman Motors Ltd Classic Cars)

It was the new, modern jet age, and what easier way to convey that than with a rocket-like, chrome hood ornament. (Courtesy Hyman Motors Ltd Classic Cars)

Yet, the biggest change was announced in April 1950, with the option of ordering the bigger 102hp, 245.6ci, L-head 'Power Plus' six-cylinder engine in the 2R5. When powered by this six-cylinder engine the ½-ton pickup truck was designated the 2R6. Unfortunately, due to the late announcement, few 2R6 versions were sold in 1950.

The front suspension was also beefed-up, and, when combined with the replacement of the lever shocks in favor of the more modern tubular type, it resulted in an improved ride and better handling.

Although the new horn button was nice, it was the eventual introduction of an adjustable fore and aft bench seat that was really appreciated, as well as some additional color choices.

Yet, the ever-growing, long list of optional equipment allowed for owners to outfit their pickup truck to their individual needs and desires.

Drivetrain equipment available included a Fram oil filter, a heavy-duty oil bath air cleaner, six blade fan, cut-in generator, heavy-duty battery and radiator, a 4-speed transmission and floorshift, overdrive, hill holder, heavy-duty and two-stage rear springs.

Work-oriented options available consisted of dual horns, a caravan top, steel stake rack, heavy-duty grille, lamp guards, twin taillights, left and right extended rear view mirrors, a spotlight, box side and tailgate steps, front splash and rear fender gravel guards, a spare tire chain with lock, and larger 6.50x16 tires.

For added comfort, style and convenience in your 1950 Studebaker 2R5 or 2R6 you could order a factory radio, heater and defroster, a standard or Glare-Proof interior rear view mirror, visor vanity mirror, a right-side exterior mirror, a rear bumper, chrome bumpers, bumper guards, license plate frames, locking gas cap, fog lamps, turn signals, engine compartment and service lights, windshield washer and wiper vacuum booster, Mattex seat covers and armrest covers, a cigarette lighter, an under-dash hand throttle, and an exhaust deflector, as well as wheel trim rings and whitewall tires through your dealer.

Total truck production of all models was 63,473 units in 1950. The Canadian Studebaker plant in Hamilton, Ontario built just 1823 of the 2R5 pickup trucks.

1957 GMC 100

Stylish ½-ton pickup trucks were all the rage by the mid-1950s, but, like the family that goes in to buy the big convertible in the showroom and leaves with the basic four-door sedan, so it was with most truck buyers. The number of styling and convenience options added was directly related to the buyer's bank balance, as well as usage.

Most dramatic and esthetically pleasing in 1957 were the ½-ton trucks from Chevrolet and its sibling from the GMC Division.

The new Chevrolet 'Task Force' and GMC 'Blue Chip' styling, first seen in 1955, had become even more refined in appearance in 1957, sporting a lighter, finely detailed, less chucky chrome front grille.

As with most GMC versus Chevrolet pickups, the front grille, badging, taillights and dash were distinctive to each. An immediately noticeable interior change in 1957 was a redesigned 'deep-cup' rather than flat steering wheel.

The '100' badge on the left section of the front grille designated this 1957 model as a ½-ton with the '150' being a ¾-ton and the '250' a 1-ton Series pickup.

Those who could afford to add to the already tasteful styling, had plenty of dress-up and paint options to choose in 1957.

This rare 114in wheelbase GMC 100, of which less than 500 were built, was fitted with an automatic transmission, the big V8 and many other of the most popular options of the day.

These included such pampering items as the automatic dash-mounted traffic viewer, factory air-conditioning, aftermarket turn signals and even a tissue dispenser.

The added eye-candy exterior options, such as the fender-mounted spare upmarket wheels and tires, and the wooden side rails provided lots of added style to this handsome Cascade Green painted GMC.

The optional V8 engine was enlarged from its

This lovely 1957 GMC 100 pickup was dressed-up enough for a typical fifties American prom night. Yet, although these traditional rear-fendered trucks were very attractive, it was the new Chevrolet Cameo Carrier and GMC Suburban pickups with their smooth, slab-sided, fenderless rear quarters that were the acknowledged leaders in high style by 1957. (Andrew Mort)

The dash design in a GMC 'Blue Chip' pickup was dramatically different from a Chevrolet 'Task Force' layout. Today, it is a quick way of telling whether or not the more desirable GMC pickup offered for sale is genuine. (Andrew Mort)

Although pickup trucks were getting fancier in the 1950s, most GMC ½-ton pickups saw yeoman's duties on farms or delivering goods. (Andrew Mort)

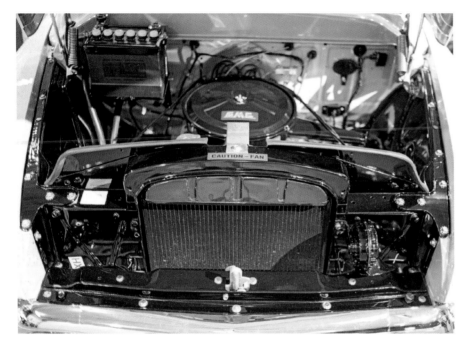

The big V8 engine was borrowed from Pontiac Division, rather than from Chevrolet, to provide pickup truck customers with another power option, and further differentiate GMC from its very similar sibling.

previous 316.6ci to a 206hp, 347ci V8, which was best in class horsepower in 1957! Standard power was a 130hp, 269.5ci Six. Rather than the standard three-speed manual, you could upgrade to a four-speed shift or, on the ½-ton only, order the four-speed Hydra-Matic transmission.

Under the hood there were other changes, but these focused mainly on the relocation of various engine ancillaries and added accessories.

High dress-up options, such as those seen here, were offered, partly due to demand, but also as tempting upgrades for buyers wanting to use their pickup for more than just work. (Andrew Mort)

1951 Mercury M-1 Pickup

While the rival GMC and Chevrolet lines differed in numerous styling cues, the Ford and low production Canadian Mercury trucks fundamentally differed only in badges, chrome accents and distinctive hubcaps. The most noticeable and important difference – especially

The family resemblance between a Ford and a Mercury ½-ton is only obvious from close up. Note the very stylish Mercury badges and trim. (Andrew Mort)

The tailgates of pickup trucks were easily removed, and thus many were lost over the years. Also, most tailgates got damaged or suffered from rust. As a result, a restored example with its original 'Mercury' tailgate has considerably higher value. Once again, the pickup bed featured a wooden floor with rub strips covering the seams. The rear tailgate was redesigned; now advertised as 'grain tight.'
(Andrew Mort)

In the early 1950s even the very basic options – such as a heater, dual sun visors and a radio – added considerable comfort, compared to earlier prewar pickup trucks.
(Andrew Mort)

The Canadian Mercury versions of the Ford trucks were very handsome and individualistic alternatives. Dressier, due to added chrome and more standard features, the Mercury trucks proved popular with Canadians.
(Andrew Mort)

Although looking almost identical, the Mercury Flathead engines were slightly more powerful than the standard Ford Flathead V8. The 1951 Flathead was also substantially different compared to the 1950, which resulted in few interchangeable parts. (Andrew Mort)

to collectors today – was the unique Mercury tailgate. Mercury trucks were sold on the Canadian market through separate Lincoln-Mercury-Meteor dealerships in the 1950s.

Although Mercury trucks were exported chiefly to the Commonwealth markets some were sent to all corners of the world. Still, production was never of sufficient volume to make it financially feasible to allow for substantial differences in the overall design.

The restyled front end design found on the 1951 Ford F1 was transferred to the M1, including the three upright, over-sized dagmars that replaced the previous simple, yet stylish horizontal bars. The teeth, with a mouth that appeared to be suffering from severe gum disease, provided a very different and distinctive look. The F1 and M1 looked wider too, thanks to the restyled fenders to accommodate the grille and inset headlamps.

Two trim packages were offered on the 1951 Mercury line-up known as the 5-Star and the 5-Star Extra.

The 5-Star Extra was a generous package that was well worth the extra cost. Included in this deluxe package were dual sun visors, wipers and horns, vent windows, added foam seat padding, added interior trim panels, a headliner, greater sound and heat insulation, added chrome hood and windscreen trim and molding, an Argent Silver finish to the large grille, two-tone upholstery, two-door armrests, a cigarette lighter, door locks, a locking glovebox, and an interior dome light.

Some of the niceties added to this rare Canadian Mercury M-1 included dual horns and mirrors, a radio, heater, wide whitewall tires, a chrome rear bumper, and runningboard steps.

Many Canadian buyers favored the Mercury version of the Ford pickup – they saw it as uniquely Canadian and more distinctive, as well as looking 'fancier' just like the Meteor car line compared to the Fords.

1951 International
Launched in January 1950, the all-new International Model L Series ½-ton pickup truck for 1951 was basically unchanged, other than the switch to external door hinges and a change in the placement of its rear-view mirrors.

In 1951, International abandoned the original concealed door hinges on its cab, and instead fitted a pair of externally visible hinges bolted to the A-post. The top hinge was also used as a mount for the side mirror, as opposed to the previous cowl mounting. (N Mort Collection)

International offered a chassis-only version so the cab and pickup box could be bought separately. A cab was ordered for an additional US$230.00, and the pickup box for just $89.00 more when purchased along with the chassis and drivetrain.

More transmission choices were offered in 1951. Buyers could order, for the first time ever, a three-speed column shift, take the standard floor-mounted three-speed shifter, or choose the more flexible four-speed, floor-shift transmission.

Interestingly, International truck production was not calculated by model year, but was instead based on the calendar year. Also, the designated year of the truck was not determined by the build date, but rather the date it was sold by the dealer to its first owner.

In 1951 the International Harvester Company also proudly announced that over one million of its trucks built since 1907 were still on the road.

The restored example shown here is a 1951 International L-Series 110 pickup, which featured the

Rearward visibility in the early L-Series pickups was hampered by the narrow, split rear window. The wheelbase of the L110 model was 115in. There was also an L-111 and an L-112 Heavy-Duty ½-ton pickup on a 127in wheelbase. The rear pickup box featured a ribbed metal, not wooden, floor. Appearing two years after Ford, Chevrolet/GMC and Dodge, and a year later than Studebaker, the L-Series finally gave International a contemporary, if not ultra-modern looking, truck. (N Mort Collection)

optional chrome twin bars spanning the wide painted horizontal grille, adding to the already distinctive look of the L-Series.

On the American-built International pickup trucks the grilles were all painted black, whereas on the Canadian produced pickups the grille was painted the body color. This rugged example was built in Canada and originally sold in Manitoba for farm use.

Optional equipment on this L-110 included a chrome front bumper rather than the standard painted black, added wooden side rails, and a side mounted, rear fender spare.

The ½-ton L-Series was available with either a 6½ft or 8ft box. The 8ft box was fitted on the longer 127in wheelbase chassis. The ½-ton models consisted of the base L-110 with its 6ft box, and the L-111 and L-112 shorter or longer wheelbase models with either the 6ft and/or 8ft box.

The L-110 had a GVW of 4200lb; the L-111 a GVW of 4500lb; and the L-112 version a GVW of 4800lb. This example is powered by its original, completely stock 100hp, OHV, 220ci six-cylinder engine.

All new in 1950 was the 'Silver Diamond' overhead valve, 100hp, 220ci six-cylinder engine. Only the ignition parts were left unchanged from the previous 'Green Diamond' Six. The engine's high torque and flexible OHV design allowed owners to pull away from a stop in high gear if need be.
(N Mort Collection)

A much appreciated dual hinge/latch hood was introduced on the new International L-Series, which allowed for better access to both sides of the engine for routine maintenance, service and repairs. Also, with both sides unlatched, the entire hood could be removed.
(N Mort Collection)

1958 Ford Ranchero

In just its second year, unique in the American market, Ranchero was already establishing itself as a style icon. It was becoming popular with all American age groups including the burgeoning youth market, thanks to such popular films as *April Love* which was released late in 1957 and starred American teen idol Pat Boone with rising film starlet Shirley Jones – not to mention the new Ranchero. *April Love*, sung by Pat Boone, became number one on the hit parade in North America, but the Ranchero wasn't as lucky.

The Ranchero on paper seemed to have it all. It

From the rear the 1958 Ranchero was virtually identical to the '57 model. Whereas the tail lights were redesigned on the car lines for 1958, the Ranchero rear end styling was the same, other than the reshaped bumper guards. (Andrew Mort)

The 1958 Ranchero dash was a carryover from 1957, other than the change in the instrument bezels. This example featured an optional factory radio and clock. The spare tire was mounted in a standing position behind the seat on the passenger side. (Andrew Mort)

featured the great style and 'personal car' image of a Ford Thunderbird, the ride and handling comfort of a Ford sedan, and the capability of an F-100. Sadly, those attributes were also its downfall, preventing it from becoming really popular in the marketplace.

True, the Ranchero had great style with its T-Bird-type grille, yet it was still seen as a truck. And, it didn't have the seating capacity or trunk of a sedan, nor was it seen as being as tough or rugged as an F-100 pickup.

Although being the height of fashion, the Ranchero

This Ranchero was powered by Ford's optional 205hp, 292ci V8 fitted with a 2-bbl carb and dual exhaust. The transmission was the standard 3-speed column shift, but with overdrive. Only 1471 base 66A Rancheros (US$2170) like this one were built in 1958, whereas 8479 Custom 66B series (US$2235) were delivered. In 1958 Ford had no competition in this niche market, but that was about to change. (Andrew Mort)

was also a practical hauler when needed, with its ½-ton load capacity. The rear bed measured 6x4.5x1.2ft for a total of 32.4ft³ of loadspace. And the subframe of the Ranchero was the same as that of the station wagon. The bolted-down floor of the wagon contained a well that could serve as an alternative or permanent spare tire location, by hinging it on one side. There was also additional room for tools. This conversion was not offered as a factory or dealer modification, but could easily be done by most garages. It then freed-up additional room behind the front seat for more secure storage instead of being left in the back under a tonneau cover.

The 1958 business recession and new legislated government credit laws in the US had adverse effects on car and truck sales in 1958. Despite looking very different and featuring new recirculating ball steering, an improved stabilizer bar, and the Cruise-O-Matic transmission when the 352ci V8 was ordered, sales fell dramatically in 1958. Offered in Standard or Custom trim only 9950 Rancheros were sold in the US.

This was a drop of more than 50 percent over 21,000 sold in in 1957, but production would bounce back to just over 14,000 units in 1959.

This fully-restored '58 Ranchero, in original factory blue and white colors, was loaded with options that included whitewall tires, spotlights and side mirrors. A 1958 Ranchero weighed 3265lb, plus ten more on a Custom series. It had a 116in wheelbase and an overall length of 202.9in with a maximum payload of 1125lb. The Ranchero had a GVW rating of 4600lb. (Andrew Mort)

Pickup truck options over the decade

From basic to bizarre

In the 1950s American pickup trucks were beginning to become more civilized, and offer additional creature comforts, instead of just optional sunvisors and dressier hubcaps. Styling cues from car lines were being incorporated to provide trucks with a corporate identity, as well as increasing pizazz. And, just like the cars of the 1950s, pickup trucks were being sold with more optional chrome and two-tone paintwork.

There were many items offered as optional equipment that today we expect as standard, even on the least expensive, very basic pickup truck.

As everyday cars became more comfortable and

It's hard to believe today that, back in the 1950s, rearview mirrors, such as this one, would be optional equipment on a 1955 Chevrolet 3100 pickup. (Andrew Mort)

The base model L-Series International pickup trucks built from 1950-52 were pretty bare bones. Optional equipment included a painted front bumper, a rear bumper, both interior sunvisors, dual electric wipers, power steering, an engine governor, an oil filter, a heavy-duty clutch, overload springs, a rearview mirror, turn signals, a dome light, and a heater and defroster. For a more comfortable and dressier L-Series truck you could add rear fender skirts, bumper guards, an exterior sunvisor, a clock, a cigar lighter, an AM radio, a lockable glovebox, a spotlight, license plate frame and antenna, seat covers, left and right door armrests, a chrome front and rear bumper, chrome door handles, a green-tinted windshield, wheel trim rings, and special paint. (Courtesy George Kirkham, Southland International Trucks Ltd)

Pictured here is a 1954 Ford V8 pickup with optional chrome rear bumper, and an aftermarket set of wooden bed stakes. (Andrew Mort)

This 1957 Chevrolet 3100 shortbox Fleetside featured the optional larger rear window, power steering, power brakes, a chrome package, two-tone paint, and tinted glass. (Andrew Mort)

Rear chrome bed rails on this '58 Ranchero added even more splash to an already splashy American ½-ton pickup truck. (Andrew Mort)

An option on the 1958 Ford F-100 was a spare tire carrier mounted inside on the box on the left side, in front of the wheel well, which made for easier access and kept it away from all the road dirt. (N Mort Collection)

A subtle but stylish addition to any fifties pickup truck was a chrome tailpipe extension tip. (Andrew Mort)

pleasant to drive, the acceptable and expected standards increased. As a result, people wanted the same standards of safety, accommodation and ease of driving in their pickup trucks.

Throughout the 1950s optional equipment gradually became standard equipment, as the pickup truck market moved steadily upward and away from basic haulers, and more towards business and family transportation.

Customers were demanding increased comfort and convenience, and this could more easily be achieved by the truck manufacturers through adding optional

equipment, which pleased the dealerships as well, as it pushed the sticker price and profit margin higher and higher in this increasingly competitive market.

Many of the options were very basic, and included items such as a passenger side sunvisor, twin mirrors, a rear bumper, turn signals, dual electric wipers, an automatic transmission, and even a heater.

Yet, even as late as 1957, the Ford pickup truck option list included such basic items as a radio, windscreen washers, an outside rearview mirror and directional signals.

Spotlamps were popular items in the fifties, and many could be controlled from inside without winding down the driver's window. Spotlamps were handy for seeing house numbers at night, or just added clarity at a time when headlamps were far from bright. Many of the really fancy spotlamps also incorporated a rearview mirror, such as the one on this 1958 Ranchero. (Andrew Mort)

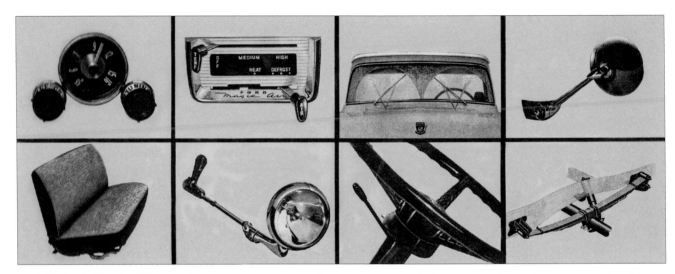

In 1958 Ford offered a full range of accessories and optional equipment. Some of the more popular options were a radio, a Magic-Aire A/C system, windshield washers, outside rearview mirrors, seat covers, a sealed-beam spotlight, directional turn signals, and heavy-duty springs. (N Mort Collection)

Added practical items ranged from optional V8-power to a dual exhaust system, bumper guards, wooden side rails, oversize tires, and larger pickup boxes.

Added dress-up items offered included a fender mounted spare, deluxe wheel discs or trim rings, whitewall tires, chrome bumpers, rear exhaust tips, fender skirts, an external sunvisor, a license plate frame, and special paint. Dodge even made its Division-defining Ram hood ornament an option in 1951.

There were some options that were aimed at purely enhancing the comfort and convenience in your pickup, such as a tissue dispenser, clear plastic seatcovers usually ordered along with the deluxe cloth interior, a cigar lighter, clock, a radio and antenna, spotlights, etc.

Then, there were some unusual options offered on pickup trucks during in the 1950s too. For example Chevrolet and GMC offered a traffic-light viewer.

And in 1952, GM was the first to introduce the automatic headlight dimmer option known as the 'Autronic Eye' on their higher-priced cars. It was then offered in 1953 in other GM vehicles. A wired-in photoresister was housed in a gunsight-like tube that sat on the top of the dashboard on the driver's side. An amplifier module was located under the hood which controlled the headlight relay via the 'Autronic Eye.' In 1958 a more compact, upgraded unit called the 'GuideMatic' was introduced with a control knob that allowed the driver to adjust the system's sensitivity threshold. Dipping often occurred due to road sign and other reflections. An improved GuideMatic was offered

GM offered a dash-mounted Traffic Light Viewer, which consisted of a ribbed plastic prism to reflect a clear image of overhead traffic lights. Because the roof extended so far forward of the driver on the dogleg, wrap-around windscreen, it was hard to see overhead traffic lights. GM bragged no stooping, squatting or squinting was necessary when stopped at a stoplight. The viewer instantly told the driver when the light changed from red to green. The prism was mounted on the top of the instrument panel directly ahead of the driver. The Traffic Light Viewer was particularly useful to drivers who fitted an exterior sunvisor on their pickup. (Andrew Mort)

The Glacier-Ice Corporation's 'Glacier-Ice' air conditioner was designed to easily mount on the passenger-side window of the cab. The outer scoop caught the air which passed through the inside container filled with ice cubes. Two vents then allowed the cool air to pass into the cab. (N Mort Collection)

These Stimsonite Safety Parking Breakdown Car/Truck AGA Flare Reflectors were sold as sets of two, or most often four. While these were aftermarket items, many truck dealers such as Ford and International sold them to their customers out of their showrooms. The Flare Reflectors were sold with warnings attached stating, "Before placing this flare upon the highway, it is important that the reflecting units be cleaned of any dust or other dirt. When placing this flare upon the highway, care must be exercised that the flare is so faced to reflect to oncoming vehicles the maximum amount of reflected light." (N Mort Collection)

There were many novel aftermarket ideas to add air-conditioning to the small pickup truck cabs in the early 1950s. A rather inexpensive and somewhat effective – for at least a short period of time – was this design by the Glacier-Ice Corporation of sunny Santa Monica, California. (N Mort Collection)

on some GM models until 1989. Later Ford offered the 'AutoDim' option, while Chrysler marketed the 'Automatic Beam Control' system.

Yet, an even more unusual option for a pickup truck was an electric shaver offered by Ford in 1957.

As well as dealer options, the aftermarket suppliers offered an almost never ending line of add-on equipment from novelty items such as skull gearshift knobs to early forms of air-conditioning.

A Toledo Wick Flare Set consisted of two or three smudge pots. A similar item was offered as the Bolser Flare Set. These Flare Sets dated back to the 1930s and continued to be used into the 1950s. The black-painted mounting bracket was used to attach it inside, or on the side of the box of a pickup truck. The all-steel Toledo Brand of the flares had a twist cover top on all of the smudge pots, so as to keep the wick from getting damaged or wet. These flares used naphtha gas, oil, or more often kerosene to keep them lit. (N Mort Collection)

Custom pickups

Back in the 'old' millennium if a truck enthusiast painted his vintage pickup a non-original color or with flames and put on a set of mag wheels it was considered a 'Custom' by many in the hobby.

In the 'new' millennium things changed considerably, and mechanical updates, minor modifications and cosmetic upgrades do not a custom make.

Many vintage truck owners have fitted aftermarket disc brakes, dual master cylinders, and so on, added seatbelts and metallic paint to their otherwise stock trucks and yet don't consider them customs. Stock wheels are still popular, fitted with modern radial tires, but equal in enthusiasm are aftermarket chrome or mag-style wheels with much larger tires.

Some might, but the majority of enthusiasts see

All of the chrome trim has been removed from this custom 1957 Chevy C10 for a cleaner look, but at the same time all that added chrome would have channelled away funds that could have been spent elsewhere.
(Andrew Mort)

The latest, state-of-the-art digital instrumentation is popular, while also being more accurate and providing a fresh, modern look, such as on this 1955 Ford. A very modern center console flows from the dash, and houses both a navigational screen and computer engine and performance read-outs.
(Andrew Mort)

these and a lot of other upgrades from the original factory 'spec' as only necessary improvements in safety, comfort and drivability on today's roads.

The term 'mild custom' was popular for a while, but this term has been used less over the past decade or so.

Yet, there is a point where the restored truck crosses the line into the 'Custom' classification. And then, in-between stock and all-out show customs, we have the 'Resto-Custom' or 'Resto-Rod.'

At first glance these pickups appear to be fully restored, original trucks, but in reality have a custom-built suspension, a far more modern, powerful engine under the hood, upgraded, new tech electronics and lavish, crafted interiors.

Pickup trucks lend themselves nicely to being

slightly upgraded while maintaining that inborn vintage look and ruggedness. And while there are lots of fully customized show pickup trucks, the majority of old fifties, slightly modified, American pickup trucks are still used for hauling, or even being driven, on a daily basis.

American pickup trucks of the 1950s are highly collectible, yet because of their intrinsic nature and sheer numbers, few are truly rare pieces.

Pickups, particularly in the 1950s, were built for use and not for impressing the neighbors, attracting the opposite sex, cruising in luxury and comfort, or for ultimate performance.

There is no rallying or racing history attached to any fifties American pickup; just a long tradition of an honest, working existence.

In most cases the personalization of a 1950s American pickup has become interpretation, and thus everything has become acceptable in today's vintage truck world.

Here are some examples of 1950s 'custom' pickup trucks – and all are driven.

Not all customs are crafted for a contemporary look. Some customizers choose a retro theme instead, such as that on this 'flamed' 1955 GMC ½-ton. (N Mort Collection)

This mild custom 1953 Mercury pickup was made more unique-looking by being lowered, a rear apron grafted on, modern polished wheels and low profile tires fitted, and the exterior sprayed bright green. Under the now front-hinged hood is a full engine and ancillaries transplant. (N Mort Collection)

A vintage truck chassis doesn't work on a custom truck. Here a 1951 Ford F-100 rolls along on a modern 'Fat Boy' chassis, outfitted with an ultra-strong Strange 9in rear end, Budnik billet wheels, four-wheel Wilwood disc brakes, and lots more. (Andrew Mort)

A stock rebuilt V8 sometimes just isn't enough. Under the hood of this '55 F-100 sits a fully custom-built V8, loaded with extra power and chrome. (Andrew Mort)

Nothing much left of the stock interior in the 1957 Chevy pickup. Almost standard equipment on a custom truck today is a full leather interior, modern collapsible steering column, air-conditioning, and a powerful stereo system. (Andrew Mort)

Not all 'customized' pickup trucks are built for show. Here's a practical 'driver' 1953 Mercury M1, rebuilt for hauling purposes, as well as for fun. (N Mort Collection)

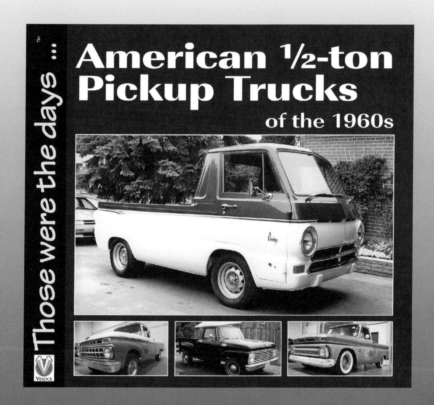

Those were the days ...

American ½-ton Pickup Trucks
of the 1960s

Following on from *American ½-ton Pickup Trucks of the1950s*, this book continues the story of the American ½-ton pickup truck during the1960s, examining its development, and including the numerous, new, alternative designs and engineering approaches. This volume also reveals specifications, industry facts and figures, and optional equipment, through detailed text and previously unpublished images.

ISBN: 978-1-845848-03-3
Paperback • 19x20.5cm • £14.99* UK/$25.95* USA • 112 pages • 150 colour pictures

For more info on Veloce titles, visit our website at www.veloce.co.uk
• email: info@veloce.co.uk • Tel: +44(0)1305 260068
* prices subject to change, p&p extra

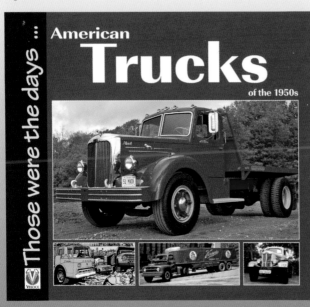

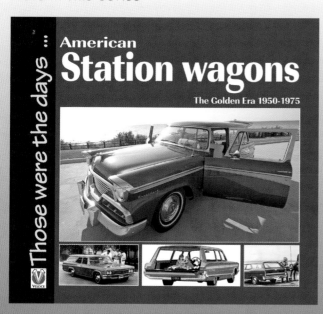

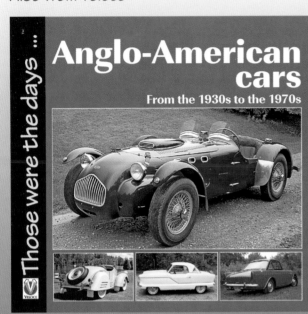

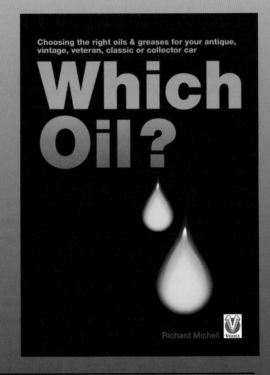

Index